MODERN WELSH POETRY

edited by

KEIDRYCH RHYS

Granger Poetry Library

GRANGER BOOK CO., INC.
Great Neck, NY

First Published 1954
Reprinted 1979

INTERNATIONAL STANDARD BOOK NUMBER
0-89609-125-2

LIBRARY OF CONGRESS CATALOG NUMBER
78-73499

PRINTED IN THE UNITED STATES OF AMERICA

ACKNOWLEDGEMENTS

The editor wishes to thank the authors and publishers who have given permission for poems to be included in this book.

Acknowledgements are due to Messrs. George Allen & Unwin, Ltd., for poems from *Raider's Dawn* by Alun Lewis; Messrs. J. M. Dent & Sons Ltd. for poems from *Gwalia Deserta* by Idris Davies, for the extract from *Branwen* by Wyn Griffiths and for poems from *The Map of Love* by Dylan Thomas; and to Messrs. George Routledge & Co. Ltd. for a poem by Mr. Alban A. Levy from *Poems from the Forces* and for poems from *The Van Pool* by Keidrych Rhys.

Poems are included from the following volumes: *The Angry Summer* by Idris Davies (Faber & Faber, Ltd.), *Poems* by Walter Dowding, *Song for Courage* by Ken Etheridge (The Gomerian Press, Llandyssul), *The Four-Walled Dream* by Nigel Heseltine (The Fortune Press), *In Parenthesis* by David Jones (Faber & Faber, Ltd.), *Poems* by Glyn Jones (The Fortune Press), *Back in the Return* by Huw Menai (William Heinemann, Ltd.), *The Ballad of the Mari Lwyd* by Vernon Watkins (Faber & Faber, Ltd.), and *The White Island* by George Woodcock (The Fortune Press).

Some of the poems in this anthology were first published in *The Bell*, *Caseg Broadsheets*, *The Dublin Magazine*, *Horizon*, *Indications*, *Life and Letters To-day*, *The Listener*, *More Poems from the Forces*, *New Statesman and Nation*, *The Observer*, *Oxford Poetry*, *Partisan Review*, *Poetry* (Chicago), *Poetry* (London), *Poetry Quarterly*, *Seed*, *The Spectator*, *The Year's Poetry*, *Transition*, *Tribune*, *Twentieth Century Verse*, *View*, *Virginia Spectator*, *Wales*, *Wales Broadsheets*, *The Welsh Nationalist*, *Welsh Review*.

CONTENTS

12

DAVIES ABERPENNAR

POEM FOR M.A.J.D.

'Dy wên yw'r pum llawenydd,
Dy gorff deg a'm dwg o'r ffydd.'

And why not? He spoke wisely.
For a bejewelled cross may sparkle with an uncanny beauty
Under moonlight, but for practical purposes
Plain wooden ones have been found more convenient.
And while Helen and Rhiannon doubtless have much
To say to Mary of Bethany and Cleopatra
While their Lady of Sorrows shakes her head and smiles,
The song of the joys of all time
Is like small coal coming out of a sieve
On a cold afternoon, unless it sings
Inside you. Here, have a peach, and see
The downiness that recedes and yet resists,
The opulence, the reserve,
The far-derived nobility, the baroque chastity,
Nature's so natural indifference to the fantasies of the geometer,
The future and the past of it,
The endeavour and mellow repose,
The well-bred classical voluptuousness,
And the good content in something done.
But try translating it for Tiresias.

TUDUR ALED

You will not find mention of her, sir,
In the obituary columns of your morning paper.
But I assure you that her passing has been marked:

13

Cilio'r lloer, cloi'r llan,
Cyfrif rhif a rhan,
Can gwin ag arian cyn ei gorwedd . . .
Iesu, wylasom,
Iesu, gwaeddasom,
Iesu, gwybuasom wasgu bysedd . . .

You, sir, have decapitated a pimple,
And the blood on your tidy tie
Suggests that despite your morning superiority
You may claim a distant relationship
To a muscular old friar who could give
A gallon of metheglin to a fishwife,
The old *Unodl Crwca.*

The fishwife can billingsgate no more,
And the phlegmatic philosopher has crawled about her,
Taking for granted her silence and her smile.
And forever still is the fair lady
Whom Tudur Aled magnificently mourned,
Her rich and far-derived comeliness trodden out
By trudge and strut and shuffle.

The servants of fashionable harlots smear
The makeshift aprons that were once her gowns.

See, sir, a supplement has dropped out of your paper—
'The Beauty that is Wales'!

POEM FOR GWYN AND KÄTHE

Join all the world's delights
Of body and of spirit,
Add to the sum all joys
Of hope, and multiply it—
I cannot think the total will exceed
The iron ration of your daily need.

14

A barge, a lull, a lapping, a soothing,
And his flaming leap sank into exhaustion.
Less lovely would she be, were she less cruel.
Let her take her leave with the decorum
Of new self-conscious friendship; let her step
Off the horizon into hazy glory
With the grace and sweet dignity
That can know no end and no endurance.

Never reach the lorn last trysting-place,
Nor cease to seek the dalliance yet unknown.
Taste not the last and loveliest of the grapes,
Nor scorn the gladdest hour as the shortest.
Touch not the stars, burn not the trembling hands,
Yet steal along the strings for melodies.

His is not the splendour of a commissionaire.
The truth he seeks is all the truth he has,
Yet, having, he must seek, for it is truth.
His is not the piquancy of a newspaper boy.
Est Ulubris. True, but you go round the world
To get there.
His is not the nobility of a romantic mediocrity.
He vindicates the right of every kitten
To chase its tail.
His is not the self-abuse of a frenzied flautist.
He makes home with Fecklessness and with Pride
Who chase the naked daughters of Shamefastness,

For you have forged the bond that makes worth-while
Ikhnaton's glance and Nefertete's smile.

POEM FOR D. ROBERT GRIFFITHS

Strew on her bloaters, bloaters—for her God
Won't mind at all—but not a bone of cod.

15

Wot doin you are of Joni bach?—
In the coal-cwtsh I be mun—
Come you out Joni bach or Ifans the preacher will call and see
you dirty as diawch—
Damo mun ay right you do say Guide me O put that milgi
diawl in the shed for to-night our Jacob.

Distinguish the existence from the essence
Of her superb swift phosphorescence.

Tomos Tin Whistle don't sing Comfort Ye like old Jenkins the
Gin do 'e?—
No mun old Tomos do only see the lines but Jenkins the Gin
did sing wot was betweeu the lines too mun

For things unspeakable already creep
About the Empress of the mourning Deep.

Wot it is I can 'ear like uffern dân let loose?—
It's the men coming from the strike meeting mun can't you 'ear
Bil Bola Mawr's voice?—
Ay to be sure mun an' fancy 'e do say aleliwia when old Icha-
bod Ifans do get the hwyl up—
Ay mun to think 'e 'ave come down from shouting aleliwia to
shouting Bust the Owners shame be on 'is dirty old bald 'ead

Gaze through the blue-green brilliance of the water
At old Leviathan's own stricken daughter.

(A sudden explosion with noise of strike agitators with howl of
greyhounds with choir in the distance singing Cwm Rhondda)

Salt is the sea, and salt the tears we shed.
Will you have fish and chips or laver-bread?

The end 'ave come our Joni see you in 'eaven with the tenors—
Ay our Jacob or in 'ell with Bil Bola Mawr

Behold the Fish of God that takes away
The stinks of all the world, now and for aye.

BEWARE, WASS

Beware, wass. A bristle-tongued generation would reduce
    The kingdom that is within you
To a dull albeit fierce protest, a bloodshot negative.
    Should we not do more than maunder:
'Why a God's name is it of more moment to us
    To strive for peace than to fulfil life,
To bite the nails for justice than to bow the knees for love,
    To secure the bare permissive conditions
Of what is godlike than to be, a brief splendour, as gods?'
Must we stiffen at last, our backs urged against the Thing?

FOR GWENHWYFAR AND BLODEUWEDD

    Hand me the comet lashing with
        Groans of desire
    Upon the aching lips of the blood-bath
        On the wheeling mount;
    For you caressed the eucharist
        In systems of Venus
    And after the muttering of the thigh
        The word of the Saviour,
Trembling upon the chalice from leagues of longing, convinces,
While Christus struts victor down the light years of the senses.

POEM FOR KEITH SCOTT

    Lust for the breezes,
        Goggle at the sun,
    Cute young Anamnesis,
        Murder's on the run.
    Grow, for the nerve of the assassin fails,
    Grow through the eggshells and the fishes' tails.

Reck not for autumn
And for winter frost,
And your own post-mortem
Glory, won or lost.
Grow, for misfortunes look the same as sins,
Grow through the ashes and the salmon-tins.

BRENDA CHAMBERLAIN

'YOU, WHO IN APRIL LAUGHED'

You, who in April laughed, a green god in the sun;
Sang in the bowel-rock below me
Words unknown, but now familiar-strange
Your voice and presence. Other quests
But led to this, to lie unseen and watch,
From cloud-ascending rib and slab of stone
Your downward passage, greendrake garmented;
A blade of wheat, watered in desolation.

O love in exile now,
I keep the hill-paths open for you; call
The shifting screes, warm rock, the corniced snows
To witness, that no wall
Precipitous, ice-tongued, shall ever stand
Between us, though we rot to feed the crow.

SONG—TALYSARN

Bone-aged is my white horse;
Blunted is the share;
Broken the man who through sad land
Broods on the plough.

Bone-bright was my gelding once;
Burnished was the blade;
Beautiful the youth who in green Spring
Broke earth with song.

TO DAFYDD COED MOURNING HIS
MOUNTAIN-BROKEN DOG

Tears that you spill, clown David, crouched by rock
Have changed to nightmare quartzite, chips of granite.
The valley chokes with grief-stones wept from eyes
New-taught that death-scythes flash in the riven block
To reap warm entrails for a raven-harvest.
Withdrawn in stone-shot gully of the barren ground;
You mourn, baffled by crevice and goat height
Proving tricksy as dog-fox run to earth in the scree,
For one who lies in company of beetle-shard and sheep,
For him whose loose dropped brain and lungs hang coldly
Trembling from the flowered ledge down ice plant ways to
        silence.
The tears you shed are stone. So leave the dead to stand as
        monument.
Be shepherd friend again, clown grinning under wet eyes,
Stopping your ears to sound the valley breeds:
A corpse-man's cry for succour, a dead dog's howl.

CHARLES DAVIES

PORTRAIT OF SEVERAL SELVES
(For B.J.M.)

I

I am persuaded now; there is no victory.
After the epic thrust, God knows
So much of misery
As brought us to dry tears,
And we had fought the whole world to a stand,
Choking the days with their dead challenge,
Blood spirting from our wounds, our hands
Quite broken and our hearts;
Then they rose up, the platitudes,
The mealy-mouthed ones,
Unnumbered multitudes,
Behind them more and more,
Still more,
The deliquescent,
A joggle of dead flesh decaying,
Sweating to ichor in the noon,
The dead, I say, rose up against us,
Armed to the teeth, the dead who are so many,
Faces of men as thick as leaves about us,
The curl of lips deceiving and deceived,
Sickening in sun-glare.
And so we fought,
And so we fell.

II

Then do not ask me why I stand and wait;
The cat-like spirit of the time with velvet paw,
Washes its face quite clean of idiosyncrasy.

The evening air grows thin,
The sky sags like a crumpled tent;
Eastward the cold world looks awry,
The leaning pillar of the light
Marks Time's last caravanserai.
There twilight holds her dusty court
On dream-world fabric of lost ground,
From the commotion of the seething air
Tears her torn banner.

                Not a sound!

III

The life I have loved has gone by.
Stephen as beautiful and stern as doom
And B.J.M. were with me.
After the fighting we were all three
A little bit merry.
Stephen in some forgotten, quiet place
Picked up a kind-eyed girl
With hungry lips,
Nor ceased from loving her
Until he saw the Queen's face, Guenever's,
Beneath the cheap make-up,
That false queen's beauty in her eyes;
Then he who started out to stem the seas
Of Arthur's loves and mysteries,
Smitten at heart, took to the pilgrim way,
The white, strange roads that run
Where once the great king ruled, in Caerleon.

IV

B.J.M. came with me.
We were here and there,
High, low, everywhere.
The midnight muster left us weary.

21

Out of the dead moment between ebb-time and flow,
The dark, distorted desert of ourselves,
On a dark day we come,
In the flaw of sudden rebellion:
Now we are fighting the waters,
Controlling the wave-heads.

THERE IS A POEM EVERYWHERE

There is a poem everywhere in making,
Typed on the white starched front
In shorthand, the symbols of its mastery;
So many signatures that in their way make plain
The splendid features of futurity
And place these epitaphs among the invulnerable slain.

There is a poem everywhere in being,
Foretelling what the frost will bring,
And sharpness of the intellectual weather;
Portents whose icy stiffness seems to threaten
A knife-edge battle, yet for that, proclaim
The eventual glory of the dawning spring.

There is a poem everywhere in breathing;
The spirit, feeding on its treasure,
Cooped in maternal darkness
Above the silence of the sheltering knees,
Drinks the dark aliment of purest sorrow
Before it ventures into ecstasies.

There is a poem everywhere in action,
Gathering the strength it sorely needs,
Until head foremost first it takes its way,
Ejaculate in life's divine confusion,
And through the steep grades of obscure rebellion
Wins to itself the beauty of to-day!

CONSTANCE DAVIES

THE FRENCH POLISHER
W.B. In Memoriam

Mr. Cowslip polished his coffins
in figures of eight,
   down-up
   under-over,
turning them horizontal
into algebraic infinites,
   long for the sides,
   short for the cover,
and beginning always
with a double curl
   at the right shoulder.

Seeing the gaslight in his workshop late
neighbours said
'Somebody's dead;
he can't be ought but coffining this time of night.
'Tis pity for him there alone,'
then with a twinge of dread
would draw their blinds and go to bed.

   Down-up
   under-over,
tracing symbols of infinity
on wooden shells of death,
between the trestles synchronizing footwork
in pas seul funereal;
he gave each one its complement of rubbers,
skipping nothing,
sparing nothing,
least of all himself,

23

although before the sun had risen twice
the gamboge cemetery clay
would turn his mirror surfaces as white as milk.

        Rich or poor
        whole or venereal
        the shine was the same,
        golden, ethereal,
warm toned as sympathy
glossy as thought—
for when you are only thirty-eight
polishing a coffin late
at night to earn your bread,
you needs must ruminate
upon the life corporeal,
how it shrinks inside its little polished nut,
a heap of bones and rag,
a bit of hair,
and if you are lucky there will be your ring
that Mr. Fox the undertaker could not twist
off your lifeless knuckle when he put you in.

        Down-up
        under-over;
now a pause to change the rubber
or to add a spot more polish—
                quick—
silence is flowing down the walls
black and sticky like the pitch inside the box;
check it with a spit
viscid and white;
it weighs as heavy in the scales as it.
        To be alive is to expectorate
        to contemplate
        to have the rhythm ache
        of figures of eight.

24

                    Down-up
                        under-over;
    outside thinking is as flawless as the shine,
    smooth as the elm
    tough resisting as the pitch,
    ignorance inviolate;
    it is the inside gnawing worm that plays the havoc,
    devouring heart,
    macerating mind,
    truth inarticulate
    knocking on the shiny shell of things, in vain.
                        To be afraid is to have pain
                        at each man's dying
                        at friends' bodies lying
    in these bloody polished boxes in the sod.

                    Down-up
                        under-over;
    come to the last sweet shine
    put on with touch as soft as angel's wing;
    no more the deep engraining
    saturating,
    thought plicating
    figures of eight,
    but melting parallels as straight
    as destiny—
                        Now let it fix;
    tot up the hours; another seven and six.
    Same pay,
    same work,
    how else can conscience lie at ease with justice?
    Why should the cheap coffin of mad Margaret
    shimmer less brilliantly
    than my lady's new mahogany bidet?
    When death reduces all to equal state
    shall Cowslip's coffins dare discriminate?

                        25

There's a laugh in that;
pick up your hat
and dout the jet;
in the little shivering hour before the dawn forget
that man's estate
comes to a bit of polish
in figures of eight—

When Mr. Cowslip died he had no shine
for elm and polishing were out of date,
but the sweetest rain that God has ever sent
fell on his plain oak coffin as it went.

NEW TRIADS

Three white things:

Y Wyddfa
in the January snows,
immaculate as thought
made perfect in a mood of exaltation.

Sea spume
frothing at the rocks,
just as the spirit decimates itself
in anger at the limits of the flesh.

Gulls in autumn
when they fly along the Straits
with russet trees for background;
so do the blenched remembrances of grief
hover to and fro across the heart,
vivid against the rust of Time.

How white is sorrow in a sinful world!

26

Three lakes:

Shadowless
as the soul of infancy,
knowing nothing of the bogs
that lie along the brim of life;
mirror bright,
reflecting only heaven;
       this is Lliwennan.

Sheltered from the keener winds,
spreading itself in ease
along the valley's flat fertility,
youth lies and dreams of victory;
but when the sun of gathering years begins to sink,
shadows steal athwart the face,
darknesses of hills unconquered, peaks unclimbed,
and the light is failing;
       so Gwynant in her evening stillness knows
       that all Eryri overhangs her heart.

RHAIADR

I am the voice of mere opinion,
surface water
scuttering down the gulleys of the mind,
I never pause,
I never think,
my torrent tongue
aware of nothing but its volubility
steals from the hills the beauty of their silence;
I have no depth,
my substance is a froth
whose every bubble word is vanity;

27

no matter what the obstacle
I push my course,
I must be heard
I must have my say;
here, where the jagged griefs of earth are dumb
I shout,
I shout until I am hoarse!
      the one
fool voice
amid these angel heights of wisdom.

IDRIS DAVIES

HYWEL AND BLODWEN

Where are you going to, Hywel and Blodwen,
With your eyes as sad as your shoes?
We are going to learn a nimble language
By the waters of the Ouse.

We are tramping through Gloucester and through Leicester,
We hope we shall not drop,
And we talk as we go of the Merthyr streets
And a house at Dowlais Top.

We have triads and englyns from pagan Dyfed
To brace us in a fight,
And three or four hundred Methodist hymns
To sing on a starless night.

We shall grumble and laugh and trudge together
Till we reach the stark North Sea,
And talk till we die of Pantycelyn
And the eighteenth century.

We shall try to forget the Sunday squabbles,
And the foreign magistrate,
And the stupid head of the preacher's wife,
And the broken iron gate.

So here we say farewell and wish you
Less trouble and less pain,
And we trust you to breed a happier people
Ere our blood flows back again.

FROM 'GWALIA DESERTA'

XV

O what can you give me?
Say the sad bells of Rhymney.

Is there hope for the future?
Cry the brown bells of Merthyr.

Who made the mineowner?
Say the black bells of Rhondda.

And who robbed the miner?
Cry the grim bells of Blaina.

They will plunder willy-nilly,
Say the bells of Caerphilly.

They have fangs, they have teeth
Shout the loud bells of Neath.

To the south, things are sullen,
Say the pink bells of Brecon.

Even God is uneasy,
Say the moist bells of Swansea.

Put the vandals in court!
Cry the bells of Newport.

All would be well if—if—if——
Say the green bells of Cardiff.

Why so worried, sisters, why?
Sing the silver bells of Wye.

WILLIAM MORRIS

Because the mind is growing cold,
A slave that bends to the God of Gold,
We have no time to learn your lay,
Sweet singer of an idle day.

We have great problems and great pains
And gas-mask drills and aeroplanes;
We would not understand your way,
Sweet singer of an idle day.

We have no frenzy in the heart,
We play a mean mechanic part—
You would not understand our way,
Sweet singer of an idle day.

We honour dolts in racing cars
And dirty dogs and talkie stars;
Our fields are brown, our children grey,
O singer of an idle day!

INTERLUDE

And now that man prepares for doom
I bring a bullfinch on my thumb,
And I walk and walk around Trafalgar Square
And up the Strand to the dusty bed of Donne
Where my bullfinch pipes in the shadow of frozen laughter,
Pipes on of health and mirth and corn and wine
In the valleys that unmated birds imagine
When flocks awake to cross the April sea.
O happy boy on my London thumb,
Sing for an hour when sunset drapes
The riverside with strange embroidery
And pipe your loudest when the placards scream
Of disasters and dictators and cinema-stars and drugs.

FROM AMMANFORD TO FLEUR-DE-LYS

From Ammanford to Fleur-de-Lys
No honest man will bend the knee
To any parasitic band
Which battens on the ravaged land.

From Dowlais Top to Swansea Bay
The men are in the sun to-day
With angry hearts and fists of fire
To meet the challenge of the squire.

From Blaina down to Barry Dock
Dai and Glyn have set the clock
That points unto the judgement hour
For the vandal in his tower.

31

SONNET

I tossed my golden anchor to the sea
To tease the twisted tides of salty joy,
And then my heart pursued the mystery
Of sea-born kings that did the moon annoy
Before the horn of summer caught the tune
Born in the shell of grief. The velvet bone
Of sea-weed forests melted in the noon
And every frond bent down to clasp the stone.
Sea-bottom surge, be gentle with my bread
For in my bread there sleeps another god
Whose hands are clean, whose heart is strong and red.
The idols of old Sabbaths loved the rod
And smiled to see our blood on window panes
And danced upon the dead in thistled lanes.

RENAISSANCE

The cocks of the south were crowing,
   And white sails shone on the sea,
And Rabelais rolled with laughter
   Under the richest tree.

Leonardo da Vinci pondered
   On the fat cheeks of mine host,
And Shakespeare whispered to Webster
   Of maids who pressed the most.

Chris Marlowe reached to the branches
   Where the golden apples grow,
And marble felt the fury
   Of Michelangelo.

O the sons of the west were singing
   And the skies of the west were fair,
And poet and painter and pirate
   Struck treasure everywhere.

Glory of sound and colour,
   Glamour of women and wine,
And the masters of music celestial
   Found the dust of the earth divine.

RHYS DAVIES

SEINE

Each ripple has been repeated before,
green yellow blue, to reappear
vague as a clinging of fingers
in a scarf of smoke, this water flowing.

Incessant, the hands of Ophelia cold
under the suave break of opals
through the muddy water stretch
to my heart with liquid fingers.

At my window the crimson velvet speaks
of tombs opening on the dark of water,
the urge to the indefinite sea. A taxi
skips to midnight. And I am alone.

LOUVRE

I would give all my old razor-blades
and a heap of sous to have her altered,
the little vacuous lips particularly,
as she stands alone, almanacked and advertised
everywhere and in a few stale words
prettily bunched by the not-to-be-accounted for
Walter Pater.

Behind her stand the eternal rocks, dark and beautiful,
as shadows for her fish-like smile,
the never-to-be-baked dough of her brow and cheeks
is Pater for the ends of the world
upon her head: and was he so subtle, Walter,
to delude so passionately?

The ascenseur is twenty centimes
to the upper floor of the Louvre.

WALTER DOWDING

I'R HEN IAITH A'I CHANEUON

When I am listening to the sweet, tuneful airs of my country,
sung by fresh and young Welsh voices that love them,
in the language so strong and beautiful,
that has grown out of the ageless mountains
and the deep, dark valleys,
I am fulfilled as I am in no otherwise fulfilled.

Then am I caught up into a realm of natural being,
and am one with my fathers,
and with them that shall come after me,
and with those who yet, in these so unregenerate days,
do speak that speech of wondrous beauty
that our fathers wrought.

WALES—A MOURNING

O once fair earth
of God-made curve and line,
How hath man raped thy loveliness

34

and brought to birth
from bestial slime,
such evil shapéd things:

All day do carrion wings
brood vulturous, over dooméd streets,
and innocents pay—
whose young fair lives
should hold but sweets—
a toll for evil dead:

O people bred in ignorance,
Lift up your eyes to see,
fair, high upon your mountains,
the glory is to be:
A land reclaimed from ugliness
a race shall be set free,
a love shall loose fair fountains
of living joy to thee.

H. L. R. EDWARDS

LUGANO, AUGUST 1937

Fire and vinegar (fir-logs and vin ordinaire)
Shattered the Alps for Hannibal, for ourselves
The clean electric clatter of forty tunnels.

We avoid the blue lips of glaciers, the giddy
Scree. Ours is the fun of zigzagging a frontier,
Italian made easy by the lovely Ticinese,

The freestone gulping lizards, the occasional bob on the
    baize, run
Specially for visitors, p.c.'s, snaps of the ready
Campanile, the panniered crone, generations in uniform

Grouped, hierarchic black blue red, on the lakeside
Waving. This is our picnic hash, to suck at pleasurably,
Content that it's tepid, salt, and at any rate out-of-doors.

MUSEUM PORTICO

This way to salvation is swept,
    Unflanked by peccant goad,
Where it is steep it is stepped,
    Plupurgatorial road.

A taxi takes one so far
    And doves escort one further
Past Hoa-Haka-Nana-Ia
    And his imperfect brother.

FROM KNEES UP, MUVVER BROWN

I

Between my thighs an extraordinary
Sun dangles, emptying light on London. The
Uncreased glacier of the Great West Road
Smooth sheen wet unwinking peels away
Before, behind zincs (corrugated), dozen tons of same,
Hold down the bucking lorry to a bumble purr
Went like an adder through Chepstow, Sid mun
(*Went tralalatere dextro too bigod!*)

Beneath my hot sore hams saddling its iron
Neck
          interior inferior
                    iron neck,
Riding cabin'd, crick in the knees,
Into the flower of cities at a throbbing 24.
Thanks Cheers Cheero Cheerho chanks

Creep up this petal to the park

Cossacks in the Row
Give many a free show.
Outofwork draper
Changing the paper
In his shoes, harrows
Overfed sparrows.
Even the gay
Squirrels are grey.

To this grimy temple,
This treed circus my compatriots come,
An afterchapel eve, decanting slowly
To their impossible Olwen, daisytracked,
The haysweet, Beaconbreasted, howletsoft,
Libations of minor hymnody.
Pembroke to Stonehenge. With bleeding nails
Lugging the holy sandstone through the scrub
My countrymen, chanting. Thence by cheap excursion
'From the playne of Salysbery to Tylbery fery'
My countrymen, hymnsinging So too I,
Fluff in hippocket, move from the openvowelled West
Up to the holy city of the Hyperbores.

They said you were dead or dying, blossom.
I have come to look at you.

IV

It is true the haggard has nested
Muting on the roof of the Mother of parliaments,
Her sons fled to the City, leaving behind
A smell of oratory. One sees her stoutest shoulders
Efficiently prop up the jewelled belly of a
Hanno, doling out a little
Back pay to the screaming mercenaries,
Mad for that Carthaginian finery. And the sane
Connoisseurs of the dropsy, doctor's chuckle:

Effin steamtugs! coo you shoodav seenum
Crawlin up ve wall:
Me tryin ter killum wiv me blowlamp
An cristiffit didn atch aht awl ve eggs!

Shades of the pulpit, you call for a
Remedy? religion revolution or beeftea?
Locked in his dripping gorge, our crimeless **Tantalus**
Knows, in Glamorgan: me Lud's town lies soft
And doesn't know it, princess on her pea.
Yet, yet the new life pushes in you, Gargamelle,
For lo, it is Piccadilly, Regent Street,
And West-End bars where passionate pilgrims sip
Sip of the passion
            passion fruit
            passion fruit juice
                        in cocktails.

KEN ETHERIDGE

ANNUNCIATION

I have seen rare sunshine held in the first birch leaves
   And the wind rearing to smell the blood of the tree,
And he has marched athwart with trumpets in the air
   And cymbals of celandine beating about His feet.

In Summer He has thrust arched breast through dark branches,
   His lips livid as campion, His breath the honeysuckle,
His golden mane live sunshine, His limbs a lion's
   Langorous with overstrength, then taut for the mating.

At the burning of autumn I have seen Him
   Crushing the vine in a wood of cypresses
And flinging a torch of disaster in bracken and heather,
   Treading proudly the corn-crop, roaring with delight.

In winter I have seen Him on the black cross of a tree
   With crows under his armpits and about his chest
Pecking with cruel beaks and eating frost.
   He suffered silently. The air mimicked his agony.

My brain replies: 'Poor fool, this is your image.
   Nature is a mirror wherein we see ourselves.
The lonely man finds mountains, the shy man valleys:
   The powerful man loves oaks, the weak man reeds.

'You make men out of trees, women from flowers,
   Boys and innocent girls out of simple grasses,
Like the Druid who made a damsel out of broom-blossom
   And flowers of the oak and meadow-sweet gathered in dew.

'Life is a lasting chaos, the world a wilderness
    Confounding little orders in devastation.'
Deny yourself then, or find Him in this black husk,
    For I can tell you, only if you know.

CARNATIONS

You Borgias among flowers, spilling so much blood
to keep your beauty dangerously bright,
there are daggers around you
pale and sharp pointed to your head
with hate and deadly love.

There is poison in your breath
from the black folds of your heart
guarding the passionate pulse of queenliness
against frivolous butterflies
that abhor you.

You shout defiance of the fear
your white sisters show,
haughtily, darkly aloof,
demons revolving into the depths of sight,
you smoulder in cardinal groups
immaculately consumed in flame
to crimson martyrdom.

SPRING FRAGMENT

The boy's green song and the lyric of youth
is a spent dream in the fingertips
of the trees.
The oak has uncurled his callow
empyrean yellow
and taken the wisdom of the sun and air
to a darker strength in his hands.

Cherry bouquet is Fragonard
pink and shadow-grey;
the blue air lights the lamps of magnolia
above gardens evening tended
where sleep the summer's roses.

What fever after youth?—Blind light or darkness,
wander in the fast of sleep through other fastnesses,
or spend a waking crying in the mountains?
Or eat the dust of wishes in bony silence?
The blood shall grow fresh wings,
not drag the old torn feathers.
Guard the crabbed-seeming chrysalis
until the Sun of every aspiring soul
touch it to beauty-life
with signal beatific.

EARLY SNOW

I saw a rose in snow,
　　The lovely late-comer
Suffered a deathly blow;
　　Winter was clasping summer.

The leaves still greening the tree
　　Pressed ice on their passion,
The bloom and the blight to see
　　Met in this fashion.

Not Winter all woe we find,
　　Nor in summer security;
Beauty is a flame inclined;
　　Death the only purity.

MASK

We are so soon dead,
The mask put aside
(The case of the living moth),
Even though delicately point carven
And gilded,
Only as dust.

Let us not indulge in the lechery
Of much used metaphor,
That unholy intercourse of conceits.
Let us be clean in language.
Let us not deceive ourselves into admiring
The fallen leaves of decadent art.
Let us be pure in the love of beauty work,
And not for ever finger the loop of flesh
That the aboriginal exults over in the still forests
Titillating with saurian wings
The swing of the loins.
Take from the vivacious tree-ladies their wit
(Dark woods built sternly on Dryslwyn banks),
And from the natural visitations—
Daisies in a cloud of sparks silver and gold,
The roses of mallow spreading,
The hair of the rain girl.
Take of all these sufficient to create
Even from flowering weeds of passion nectar,
And crush the inherited apple of the world
In a merciless fist,
Like the norm of change pressing the shell
Hanging under the eaves of mossy heavens
Until the earth burst with sky-wings.
Look to that and love not too much
The mask whose eyes will soon be black hollows.

AN OLD COLLIER

His face like parchment skin with many a scar
  Traced in blue lines of coal, eyes sad and dim,
As of a saint fixing his cross afar
  Beyond the world that has no grief for him
And little joy in some old book of Hours
  Yellowing in minium frame. No light of laughter
Nor the dark brine of tears' cleansing powers
  Can flavour the design of his hereafter.
The crossed veins of his knuckles, knotted white
  Are like the ivy's agonies of root,
And scarcely can his back still stretch upright
  From earth that is fast growing to his foot;
And even when his body feeds the grave,
His soul is mastered by the iron slave.

DAVID EVANS

POEM I

The cotton-still spire cracks in chimes on the
Televised air. From gullet spins a chute
Of pigs-crews and keysigns, filling the air
With vibrations like a holy fork. The clock wilts

In its cell, the tower overbrimming its last ticks;
It acts as metronome to the anthem swan-song
Quarried by idiot. Outside the frost chatters
Meagre bones on the grave-slabs in saxhorn call.

Brown blood is congealed on the yew trees
In this dead egg-glass eternity. Brown
Blood is poked on the cottages for ever as they
Nudge their way like beldams along the twisted

43

Chassis of the guttered street. We are governed now by
Perfumed fish-cats only. We scratch the separated air
For the right pew in the darkness, for our amateur
Power-station works only on Saint David's Day.

POEM II

Screamlight streams of gleaming waterbreasts smiling
At their river-washing in cathedral panes,
Gorgeous jungle-wine in buckets slipping further
Down vague avenues of aspirin canes.
Bellied snakes there in plenty in the
Eyeless swamps in this congested paradise
Sipping-in deep-chested ease, death's luxuries.
At inventing gaudy colours disease curls in every flower
Turning fruited shoulders to the yellow heat.
All this geranium hothouse wonder
Has mild Welsh mutton at sour meat.

SONA DIALECT

Gettown fro their you
break for your whipcords
if yor dunnot gettown
hau casol for the jawl bach.

gum, wheezie creekie, tellum a story
of Corris and god's big gutter.

oh behewtiful, yes yes the pickcutter
llan of Pwllgwaelod . . . . .

llan, llan always mam
Mam a good whilber-ful mam.

jawl gettown by there willewe
heil give it story orright
crack your stick, willewe, defile
you crack neck meboy
munjawl all always wears in this Wales.

SYNTHESIS

Broken as a clown's sunshade
The mood churns inexpressibly
In the bungaloid patch, fingered
By caterpillars. It is held
Like the gunned rabbit
Sail-riddled
Chipping the earthenware bits
With the thick cabbage-stem
Of growth. It is the nucleus
Of world.

THIS POLITICAL TIME-PLOTTED DAY

This political, time-plotted day
Has clotted my dying dream;
Dream evil—grandfathered
Once by a country clock.
Where there was freedom then
To slope like a secret mammal
Uncountered, hanging a ribbon
High up in the highest tree.
Or to taste the unhurrying wheat
Of what timeless sowing? But now
The calendar is out, and the moon
Frightens all but the eye-lust
Of this mountain owl.

Once I would stroll unlonely
By the saw-edge of the forest
Past the weir-pool and through
The mists always in the evening
Or with the four hours of the wind.
The warm day needs company
And pleases only the southern tooth
But the tongue-searching night
Brought a stillness which outshone light
And a calm which stirred louder
Than the winds of Garn Goch.

Now when I see
The lame child prettily
Playing scotch of the flagstones . . .
. . . Or post a letter taken
From an arm-locked book . . .
Now when the word of the sun
Searches for the unprofitable goose
Of Garn Goch's red shoulder
And all else is the same
My only joy is outside time,
Untangling the place from the moment.
Like an apprentice ghost I search
For my own identity in the fields,
And contemplate the widower moon
Scoring the unmerciful hills.

GEORGE EWART EVANS

AT THE SEASIDE

Froth on the lip of a crescent sea
proudly preening on promenade
assault of sea on windy rock awaring
the moments sporting as with splash of spray.

there snatches wrinkled-neck grey-suited
paper that tells him if his money-cakes are burning.
flat-slippered shuffles to deck chairs facing sun
the weight of years and paunches bearing down
ineffectual gaze at flesh that flaunts it by.
high-conscious they sit behind the hydro sunglass
at ease to view with vague forebodings.
coming to tea with honey and sun-burned arms.

What comes after this? where turns the wheel?
no longer hold our corner of the sun?
. . . Fear is left with sugar at the bottom.

POEM

Progress in the peaceable blue of a sky in summer
cloudy mists and promise of high dominion:
to dream with back-thinking speed
foretaste of domed content.
Colour focuses, brings all to a point,
to a real hereafter.

Not for us: the struggle is to the still-beyond-the-clouds.
Viewed from above field-ordered affairs
neat hedged without the thorns
and geometrical trees that mock not
and point not to a blank sky.
No perchance dreaming.
It stands with feet on earth for climbing. . . .

Four bombers with intermittent drone
crash through the hope-screen:
pulse-menacing boom of human engines
red-bedaubed blue, crimson red
with vesicles and gas-bleared eyes:
sky raining mortal earth:
each cloud an eye that accuses and mocks
white-faced wonder and dismay speckles. . . .

Crystal waters to a waiting world are gone.
Soul is the muddied surface of a dark pool
And depth is only deep in its confusion.

We can no more sit on the bank
Expecting the ripple of a smooth image.
The light flung stone of conjecture
Will no more cause the folding of the circular waters.

CHARLES FISHER

PREOCCUPATION WITH DEATH

Swiftly ending their stories, feeling
The guitar's weight urgent on the silk knot,
Minstrels have skipped the more irrelevant adventures,
Reaching beyond the last cadence, the death of the hero,
To the applause, quick and credulous, the certainty of supper.

But the rough company, come at first with reluctance
From field and stable, or the distraction of drawing-rooms,
Have waited blankly, full of pity and premonition
Stunned with the clubs of grief to read in his face
A fuller promise, a more complete assurance
That failure was only temporary, a retrievable error.

And the singer, knowing his task, obediently
Chooses a brighter chord, compels the illusion
With the familiar pledges, the supernatural
Return to victory, the discomfort of enemies.

Serving a necessity he invents the future
That men may sleep untroubled by old disasters;
Complacent in virtue: nevertheless he is troubled, knows
The hero will not return; that story and death were final.

SOME PRODIGIES

Mozart, a lorgnette's target, child without toys,
Consumed utterly by his own costly gift,
Disdaining the dancers by his precocity
Was rewarded at length with a formal curtsy.

Jesus of Nazareth, wise as miracles,
Instructed priests in childhood, and he died
Crucified and forsaken cruelly.
Stars, angels, kings, surround his nativity.

Athenian boy, swift master of hexameters,
Frail voyager through dreams, Thomas de Quincey
Sleep soundly now. Time to your tomb has sent
Laurel and poppies both for ornament.

Nelson walked placidly through the dark wood
To find his parents; oh, he felt no dread
Of owl, or hooded ghost. For lacking fear
Men shot him down, put blood on his Admiral's gear.

Beset by sanity and climate, another
Outwitted both, though sly and preoccupied
With writing; for men weep, having quite forgotten
The lives of Kings, the death of Chatterton.

Between the uplifted bow and the fired string
Is time to note these several prodigies.
Cease, now. The work begins. People are looking.

WYN GRIFFITH

NEW YEAR'S EVE

Is there a song for the New Year
With its great load of months? A slow song
Dragging its way through notes low and long
A hard song with a thump of fear, a little trill
Of hope quavering, uncertain, shrill.
Call it a dirge. There will be death,
Want, much to lose, doubt: but the weak breath
Of wonder will grow strong, and there is hope also
Who knows what birth? No dirge but a glow
Of music with silver streak of trumpets breaking through.

And the Old Year? Sing loudly:
A dribble of hours and nothing more but release,
An end of striving. Come spend the last coins gaily
Throw these farthing minutes to buy peace,
For we are rid of a great burden of months weeks days,
Of sadness, pleasure turned dry in the mouth, pride undone . . .
But there was joy, a finding of new ways
On old hills and warm rain veiling the sun.
Sing not so loudly, gladly.
I have lived darker years and I know not . . .

Good night, good morrow.
The bells are ringing in a sky of stars.

FEBRUARY NIGHT

Seeking the prow of thought piercing the black
beyond the quick landscape of fashion,
waiting to hear the bell buoying the track
where to-morrow waits the new vision:

astride this uneasy moment pride beckons
a weak remnant of memory to strengthen
nerves deadened by use. Starving quickens
the mind surfeited by mass production.

until the sinew droops and the will tires
of the mere choice of many likenesses:
so that now remembering the glow of fires
lit by forgotten men in dark places

I can resist all striving for an issue,
knowing that fulfilment is but a knot
of hardness in the surrounding tissue,
a word in a dream this sunken night.

Future and past, then, merged in a tremor
and the weight of the world against the morning:
there is an echo from a distant summer . . .
who call it laughter must reject its meaning.

MADAM RUMOUR

Here, now, in this huddled time
With madness driving fear, smoke on the gun's lip,
clatter and dodder in the air,
courage they cry, brave men be bold
look right look left across the sea
stand to the ramparts of your great estate
here, now, in this dowered land
where children grow to idleness and youth dies
into empty days upon the pavement, here.
    I saw the moon hungry and a star pale
    above the wood, but no-one called,
    no exhortation in the falling wind.
Pursuing splendour into dust
bring vanity to walk the street:

men die but once and hunger stays.
Want carved this face, so little left to death.
Loud words upon a silent sheet:
No answer, Madam?
    None. No, none.

POEM

If there be time enough before the slaughter
let us consider our heritage
of wisdom, remembering the coil of laughter
girdled our youth, wine of bright vintage
carrying short sorrows into oblivion;
some talk of love in smooth meadows
where dusk brings quiet and night a vision
of daylight joys freed from their shadows.
Above all, wisdom: for years are shrinking
into a huddle of days and the world a parish
where neighbours bolt their doors and lights are
    dimming.
Soon there will be nothing left for us to cherish
but the grave words of the last statesmen
before the battle starts and the air is darkened:
fast fall the night upon the frightened children
and on the wombs where once they quickened.
What towered land of man's endeavour
will first be desert, with all our learning
a burnt page trodden in the dust of error?
Farewell to wisdom and to all remembering.

EXTRACT FROM 'BRANWEN'

I have borne too long this burden
pressing the fibres of my heart into pain.
Old tunes and the green-mottled grey rock
above the bay drawn in a curve bow-taut,

old tunes and a cloud
from Snowdon driving valley-light over hills
to this dark headland. There is a castle now
upon Harlech old as a forgotten dream
but I cannot see it
nor with the touch of its worn stone
bring into life new thought new music new desires.
An old tune with the wind sharp as a harp-rustle
counterpointing this day into centuries of words
of notes of all I half-remember, old tunes, old tales.

Is there no escape?

No ease of this burden until I cast
each stone of this castle beyond the day
far into time unspent and with each stone
the lamentation of a brood of men who heard,
oh! and stood beyond their grief an instant
silent at your name, Branwen, Branwen.

SILVER JUBILEE

Faint now in the evening pallor
answering nothing but old cries,
a troop of men shouldering their way
with a new tune I recognize

as something near to Flanders, but far
from the dragon years we killed
to no purpose, scattered seed
on land none but the devil tilled.

That a poet sings as his heart beats
is no new word, but an ancient tale.
Grey shadows on the pavement
and Europe sick of its own bale.

I have no answer, no rising song
to the young in years who are old
with our arrogance, our failure.
Let it be silence: the world is cold.

ALL SAINTS

The processes of death abound,
They smear the sky, the ground
Is stained a deeper red than Autumn knew.

Beyond the fear, the grief;
The stolen lives too brief
To mould the fashion of the years they gave.

God comfort all who wait,
And free their minds of hate,
Let sorrow burn the dross, let wisdom rise.

This festival is ours to hold
Who sent the Young to meet the Old.

PETER HELLINGS

FROM DISTANT LANDS

(*For the writers and artists of Europe who have been
forced to leave their own countries*)

From distant lands
They have come,
Across centuries held in the grip of murderous hands,
Leaving the bitter mirth
And mock heroics of the drum.

In the clear air
Of this town
A painter of men and women is caught in the flare
Of the great grief of the earth
Like workers breaking stone.

For the blood and the bone
Have returned
Like African fetishes or the burial of a nation's sun,
And under the threat of death
Pictures and books have been burned.

The lives of men
Are destroyed
And neither courage nor cowardice can remain
The reason for drawn breath,
But only what is enjoyed.

In distant lands
They will dream
Of lives like lovers spreadeagled on blazing sands,
Aware of their own birth,
Flaring in heroic time.

SYNTHESIS, ABOVE SWANSEA

I

Dribbling like a scribbled word to the seashore
rain indecisive beating no body rose
no brackish jackal
levels to criticize no pistol.

The tower swivels no searchlight eye
no juggernaut jewel
whose hands lie black and heavy
like dead birds on a corpse;

the gaslight crabs claw the sand;
the rigid station sags.

Laughing, mock wind twining round a lamp-post.
The craters of smoke
fired in a violent upheaval are cut and ripped by cogs.

Dribbling like two scribbled words to the seashore
the question strains the hyphen.

Put the gas out
it kills its crabs;
feet will pass over
towers. And seers are vital.

II

Spring come, the young
plants inch upward in stealth like young kings
now. And memory is a filament
fused, backchat from the back row.

All now point to the west road acute faces
with the bucking wheel of luck
and empty cases;
and we march in a mass to where the stream is
fast as a new-world girl who never loses caste.

In the city vain the summer
wins, and winter's drummer gets
a drumstick for his pains.

The wealth of wonder in our ritual blood is
this burning hair bright
like burning wood.
In the barbarous city we
all honour Spring
for what it's worth.

Grey to-day, hear the wind torture
the grass.
We stand doubtfully aware of
our helmets or
of ever waking up from the nightmare.

We do not smash this glass
murderer with a gorgon's grief
we do not swivel giant eyes and turrets
till he dies.

We stand
are stork
we fondle and force the sun and her visions
who walk on the iron fortress
spiking guns and clocks.

The sun which cannot be
darkened or aureoled by man
shall never be assailed.

STUDY: FOR EZRA POUND

(From a portrait by Wyndham Lewis)

Slanted faces of men
In a world of thought,
Beside their newspapers, under windy sun
An instinct for beauty:
Translators note
High traces of forgotten rapture in the silken **dragon.**

57

Slanted rays of the sun
Illumine like cynic faces
The colourful world of desire, and over the vivid land
Where the bitter ambitious beauties
Rock and moon in the wind
The dangerous intentions of their day draw to an end.

Slanted faces of men
In a world of hate,
Beside their histories, on various planes of thought,
Kissed by long rumours
Of falling cadence talk,
Low voices of exultation that the winds distort.

SWANSEA MARKET

I walk like a legend through cathedrals and markets
Of this pastoral land
Where seeds of flowering fruit the nerves reflect
And the cheap is suspect.

Here labour like spare plants out of a dry rot
Dai and Megan of the oak,
Whose lives will burn out like a brilliant wisecrack
In storms of talk.

Their stone is carved by a changing weather of time
Eroding the green hearts
And faces drawn with endurance, till it hurts
Enough to commit a murder

Or to start stripping themselves to the skin just for relief
Like a frightened flower;
To begin drinking in the lean heretical power
Of a goat or a thief.

Here should flourish the active praise of life
In action,
The silent lyrical courage of plant and sun
In soil and birth.

But cheap rhapsodic fragments are whirled and spin
In a wild ironic dance.
The golden fleece of the earth is seared with vengeance
And hero is heroin.

FAIRYTALES

At sunset under the low clouds, clustered like rocks
In this wined landscape of love and lemonade,
A green
Girl from Gwalia shaking out burnt-cork locks,

The sun and moon in the sky at the same time,
In the distance the sugar madmen dance among damsels
In a brown-corduroy atmosphere,
Coloured marionettes breasting lightheartedly the amber risk.

Strolling along pavements of papier mâché, like lost tulips,
In distorting mirrors of desire we catch the eye
Of a jazzy bizarre beauty,
The green tailed the dragons in a dumb daft sky.

But now the significant lighthouse, the sleeping cars,
Whose draughty castles puff into a silent flame,
Whom we have seen before
When all our neon lamps were merely lighting,

All these are coloured magic, fairytales,
Of phantom knights who turned out to be real,
And we
Are tipsy wizards chanting over Wales.

ROBERT HERRING

NO NICE GIRL'S SONG

As a woman who stands on an echoing beach,
    alone, distraught, forlorn
seeing a ship bear beyond her reach
    her noblest of men born,

I watch you go where never can I follow,
    sulkily further from me.
I am left watching, waiting for days to swallow
    all that is sick in me.

When I turn back, old things are unfamiliar
    now they recur alone.
Only feared future's friend, being full of you,
    from whom the past has grown.

Sure, every day will make both these seem frailer;
    I know if you return
it may be as a sea-enfranchised sailor
    whom lands and sub-loves burn.

You will have done so much—perhaps—without me.
    So many your days will fill.
Or if they don't, it will be worse about me,
    who stand in this day still.

Naturally, there will be no note of one still giving
    only a self outgrown.
Views change. In me will be small living
    for you, in what we'd known.

SIEGE CONDITIONS

We may not say
now
what we see,
lest each day
cow
us not to be.

We learn to watch
dismemberment
without a catch
or membrane rent.

Spurt, split and trickle—
life is death.
We die;
and, sickening back to breath,

assume what's no more,
has not been.
Scorn obsequy
for what's obscene.

Suave
is the bravery
that denies
fright. But the sights
have erased eyes.

POEM OF QUIETNESS— 2
II

Through centuries of cyclists' traffic-blocks,
turning to woods whenever red runs green;
through years' 'take cover', never once 'all clear',
and pushing 'out' doors always going 'in';

through dreaming actuality, not real,
and waking anguished on week-ended towns;
through pavéments prising into Everest hills
and shrines whose priests are barmen-after-hours,

let the world rattle. Let it stop. Let's hear
sanity tapping through the blind man's streets.
Meet ourselves in milk-bottles and return
to dawns condensed in soup-cans, slicing thumbs
by final embers, with the ash-tray full,—

Out of the howling quiet, peace drums in.
Out of the laundry sky, some colour comes.
You, when the stars pale, stir the fire in me.
At last you stand there, unexpectedly.

'*You see me now as you must know I am.*'
Kicking the fire, 'Yes'
                    '*Good*'
                            'It's very cold'.
A river tug upbraids some cock to crow.
'*Now am I as you know that I must be?*'

Now I can see you!—'Yes, I know—you *are*.'
Brown fringe of grey coal fritters the last red.
'*I have come through a non-Arabian night.
Peter I've been without a fire. My fight
was not like Jacob's, lacking you to fight.*'

'You see me still as lover'
                        '*Yes.*'

'You have not changed. Nor I.
Your journey fails.'

That was the answer given by me to one
who came as answer, was the voice
that lit all stars and set ablaze my town,
making dream indistinguishable from life
in all but time,
being before or since, too little
or too much; as life is.

POEM OF QUIETNESS— 3
III

An ache is easy. Longing's length
soon we can settle in its grave;
share it, maybe.
           One can behave
quite quietly, when loud the cry.
Heart ate by worms, bright is the eye.
Love's hellth I know.
           But new, this strength
that feels it is alive, while yet
all other feeling I forget.

CHELSEA CRYPT

(*Lines on first learning how little was left
for burial after fire-bomb and water-bucket.*)
      Crashes made these ashes,
          turned
      from structured bodies
      to bones, burned.

      Not a limb now. Scarce
          a shred
      identifiable
      as dead.—

Put the fire out.
            Pour
the can. Drown men's
charred rebuke to Man.

Pounded; battered; cowed
            in crypt,
flailed by fire and
water-whipped,

these, dismembered by the
            main's
direct hit, go down
the drains—

hiding, hurt; now safe,
            not sound;
home again by
under-ground—

Seat for Sadie! Room for
            Fred!—
but which of these
is those who're dead? . . .

Liquidated, lives that
            burned.
Now to Thames their tide
has turned . . .

Down the gutters dowse
            their veins.
In my head remain
their brains.

Flow on, fleshless. Ghosts,
                    yet real . . .
While dust we are,
Yours,—I make steel.

NIGEL HESELTINE

EPITHALAMION

(For K. R.)

So parc has a gate!
and the opening pump straight-handled new varnished
stoned boned fronts of plas and fferm too
strand-brand themes for the water-weaver
propped in the carnival cart with the
Minister (finished here) Llan sant
Llan sancteiddier.

Bowling bells!
Tomb-tubes of organist-feet stop Vox Joanna
see starter and setter now-sleuthed altar
stopwatch in hand
pass those clasped archives of springing name
to the bell and candle of Keidrych's
munition scheme, skein. Percussion
bog, bird, gwdihw.

THE FOUR-CORNERED TOWER:
LLANYBRI

This is a surplus in a four-cornered
four-cornered tower

      lung drowned
crisp air and fair houses
parked in the slated few
rib-ridged gardens manse
piled rubbish allotments

A mile from the sea where the sea
from there to Brazil floods with the tides

This wicked man
like a black cat biting his thumb

The burning shawl on the tower
swollen by springing yeast entices
the naked ships
over the country harrowing their crew
with patched victuals.

The crude parson bound in china cat
fell on the door-jamb

Black cut your seven lamps
no wick no oil
to grow in punts this war.

DENBIGH EISTEDDFOD

11TH AUGUST 1939

An old man speaking of poetry
gave us no crown no chair
no father no mother no voice
for to-morrow

for to-morrow death for to-morrow
death (nobody's seen it easy, to say
death); for to-morrow (if we're sober)
maybe a crown.

The crowd wilted and muttered, the old man
cleared his right hand of the air,
his white hair in disgrace
cleared from the stage

speaking to poets in danger, 1,200 poets
hooted and hissed when that old man
gave them no crowns.

HERO OF HIS VILLAGE

Though you are missing from the shelf
where your family coffins rot in the vault,
your cross is on the church wall
decorated with a button or two from your coat.

So the children coming with the hymn-
books in their hands see that you died
for liberty or some cause and hang
above where the parish magazine is displayed.

Though there is nothing of you but the buttons,
those in the cricket-team you taught to bowl
remember you; the girls you looked aside from
lest you become entangled, married now
look beyond their solid husbands, remember you well.

Though you left no child, nor a wife
nor ploughed land save once on leave
as relaxation; though the parson leaving
his church in a hurry now never sees
your cross, yet given a proper occasion the man
could preach a sermon on your dying that would make
futile in comparison the longest life.

AT FIRST

The flower is the forest: behind the mountain
a ravine, the south sun
by our walking, our leaping, warmed,
calmed the spined gorse: the flat sea
spread for us.

The mountain, the joy, the man in his field:
your hair in the gold light, your
body curling in the sky, on the line of the ridge leaps
on the mosses and flowers, we laughed then
when we ran.

At first shy then the lips cling
like creeper, joy running in the throat, in the bowels,
the folding hands, dis-similar, live;
in the pupil is darkness, wide iris
looks searching.

I have you in the crook of my arm as the sinking
sun floods on the sea, the grey ship sticks
on the ebb-tide, pied duck fly
over our close heads as the dark comes
on the purging, the burning.

GORSE

Eared flower blue yellow pricks
spined heather the round hill:
in a cleft, chasm, the linnet
scrapes some music; words
shooting and searching, the pied
sycamore leaves first.

Eared yellow heavy on
spines spread yellow and hawthorn
more mass weight bare green
spikes spinning, here high desire:
gorse is in flower and kissing
perch on drab lips spines prick
this kiss is blood.

Yellow is heavy on skin the spines
bear down the bloody crown; skin
stretched before thin tears red
splash, in the yellow scrape the linnet
stones frequency call clear in drowned
peat water stream, gorse and dry
blood by this road.

The spine is the spear bare
by eared yellow flower will follow
here in month's joy fresh as green
is the gate's way to green hollow.

WANDERER'S NIGHT-SONG

You who have the horse can ride
down to the sea to the edge of the tide,
I have a barking in my ears
dogs at the gates
discourage a man that waits;
to-night I sleep with my fears.

You who have your wives can hide
in her broad breasts and under her side,
I have the tough turf and a stone in my back;
They shudder at the cold returning
to their wife's bed at two in the morning,
I crook my frame under a sack.

BARTER OUR NORTHERN DARKNESS

Can you picture the decision
that will free us beyond the day?
the size of the night is an orbit
beating below households.

O singer who treads the bare
rocks of the south, barter
our northern darkness for your
stinging song that breaks the houses.

EMYR HUMPHRIES

1536–1936

Will you come back?
The sky is burning
And the hills are angry,
In the ferns there are
Wrathful whisperings—
Spirits grow tired of waiting—
Four hundred years upon a rock
Of disappearing Hope—
Freedom, will you not come back?
Our souls are Hungry!

UNLOADING HAY

Unloading hay, a tumbling heavy summer task,
Thrusting the pitchfork down in the dried-up piled-up ungreened
This unexperienced and soft hand of mine will harden (grass,—
So I hope, in lifting each loose load with each tight grasp
I take upon this polished pole. This hay is not
So light and cloudy as perhaps it looks from the hill.

Its content is both rough and hard. Dead thistles
That preserve their bite, hard hay, hoar bits of hedges even.
Heaven can be no soft and easy place, but surely
Full of the country air, hard work, and other country customs.
And is not the quivering town all nerves no muscle,
Rush, fear and never ending fuss a little counterpart of Hell?

SYMPATHY EXPLAINED

When Mrs. Evans died they sang
She had a saintly soul,
But well those two-tongued neighbours knew
Her heart was black as coal.

A withered heart—a poisoned heart
Within a woman lay,
That never would be purified
Until her flesh turned clay.

I know now why those neighbours cried
Upon the funeral day.
Those tears were all for their own selves
So soon to pass away;
They felt their blood a-growing cold
Upon that funeral day.

A NONCONFORMIST

I was not meant to kneel at the cool High Altar,—
My palate is too coarse for Holy Bread,
Vestments for me are cloaks against the Almighty,
The arresting song of boys is merely song,—
Rather made to pick up an old magazine
One evening when it was early for bed
And casually read an article of Faith

Which for a moment completed my faint picture
Of Jesus silently pointing at my courage:
'Follow me in the face of hostile crowds
Weapons, derision, hatred, scorn, follow me
From Gethsemane, from sweat to blood, to the horrible Cross
To look down at the will of God
In a drunken, jostling, swearing, filthy mob.'

DAVID JONES

THE FIVE UNMISTAKABLE MARKS

Ivenimus eum in campis silvae
and under every green tree.
Matribus suis dixerunt: ubi est tricticum et vinum? Cum defi-
cerent quasi vulnerati . . . cum exhalarent animas suas in
sinu matrum suarum.

The memory lets escape what is over and above—
as spilled bitterness, unmeasured, poured-out,
and again drenched down—demoniac-pouring:
who grins who pours to fill blood and super-flow insensately,
pint-pot—from milliard-quart measure.

In the Little Hours they sing the Song of Degrees
and of the coals that lie waste.
Soul pass through torrent
and the whole situation is intolerable.

      .   .   .   .   .

And the place of their waiting a long burrow,
in the chalk a cutting, and steep clift—
but all but too shallow against his violence.

Like in long-ship, where you flattened face to kelson for the
shock-breaking on brittle pavissed free-board, and the gun-
nel stove, and no care to jettison the dead.

No one to care there for Aneirin Lewis spilled there
who worshipped his ancestors like a Chink
who sleeps in Arthur's lap
who saw Olwen-trefoils some moonlighted night
on precarious slats at Festubert,
on narrow foothold on le Plantin marsh—
more shaved he is to the bare bone than
Yspaddadan Penkawr.
    Properly organized chemists can let make more riving
power than ever Twrch Trwyth;
more blistered he is than painted Troy Towers
and unwholer, limb from limb, than any of them fallen at
Catraeth
or on the seaboard-down, by Salisbury,
and no maker to contrive his funerary song.
    And the little Jew lies next him
cries out for Deborah his bride
and offers for stretcher-bearers
        gifts for their pains
and walnut suits in his delirium
        from Grays Inn Road.

But they already look at their watches and it is zero minus
seven minutes.

      ·   ·   ·   ·   ·

      Riders on pale horses loosed
and vials irreparably broken
an' Wat price bleedin' Glory
Glory
Glory Hallelujah
and the Royal Welch sing:

Jesu
            lover of me soul . . . to *Aberystwyth*.
But that was on the right with
the genuine Taffies
            but we are rash-levied
from Islington and Hackney
and the purlieus of Walworth
flashers from Surbiton
men of the stock of Abraham
from Bromley-by-Bow
Anglo-Welsh from Queens Ferry
rosary-wallahs from Pembrey Dock
lighterman with a Norway darling
from Greenland Stairs
and two lovers from Ebury Bridge,
Bates and Coldpepper
that men called the Lily-white boys.
Fowler from Harrow and the House who'd lost his way into
this crush who was gotten in a parsonage on a maye.
Dynamite Dawes the old 'un
and Diamond Phelps his batty
from Santiago del Estero
and Bulawayo respectively,
both learned in ballistics
            and wasted on a line-mob.

Of young gentlemen wearing the Flash,
from reputable marcher houses
with mountain-squireen first-borns
prince-pedigreed
from Merionedd and Cyfeilog.

C. of E. on enlistment eyes grey with mark above left nipple
probably Goidelic from length of femur.
Heirs also of tin-plate lords
from the Gower peninsula,

detailed from the womb
          to captain Industry
if they don't cop a packet this day
nor grow more wise.
Whereas C.S.M. Tyler was transferred from the West Kents
whose mother sang for him
at Mary-Cray
if he would fret she sang for lullaby:
          We'll go to the baltic with Charlie Napier
she had that of great uncle Tyler
Eb Tyler, who'd got away with the Inkerman bonus.

     .   .   .   .   .

The trees are very high in the wan signal-beam, for
whose slow gyration their wounded boughs seem as malig-
nant limbs, manœuvring for advantage.
   The trees of the wood beware each other
               and under each a man sitting;
their seemly faces as carved in a sardonyx stone; as
undiademed princes turn their gracious profiles in a
hidden seal, so did these appear, under the changing light.

For that waning you would believe this flaxen head had for its
broken pedestal these bent Silurian shoulders.
   For the pale flares extinction you don't know if under his
close lids, his eye-balls watch you. You would say by the turn
of steel at his wide brow he is not of our men where he leans
with his open fist in Dai's bosom against the White Stone.

Hung so about, you make between these your close escape.

The secret princes between the leaning trees have diadems
given them.
   Life the leveller hugs her impudent equality—she may pro-
ceed at once to less discriminating zones.

75

The Queen of the Woods has cut bright boughs of various flowering.

These knew her influential eyes. Her awarding hands can pluck for each their fragile prize.

She speaks to them according to precedence. She knows what's due to this elect society. She can choose twelve gentle-men. She knows who is most lord between the high trees and on the open down.

Some she gives white berries
                some she gives brown
Emil has a curious crown it's
                made of golden saxifrage.

Fatty wears sweet-briar,
he will reign with her for a thousand years.

For Balder she reaches high to fetch his.

Ulrich smiles for his myrtle wand.

That swine Lillywhite has daisies to his chain—you'd hardly credit it.

She plaits torques of equal splendour for Mr. Jenkins and Billy Crower.

Hansel with Gronwy share dog-violets for a palm, where they lie in serious embrace beneath the twisted tripod.

Siôn gets Saint John's Wort—that's fair enough.

Dai Great-coat, she can't find him anywhere—she calls both high and low, she had a very special one for him.

Among this July noblesse she is mindful of December wood —when the trees of the forest beat against each other because of him.

She carries to Aneirin-in-the-nullah a rowan sprig, for the glory of Guenedota. You couldn't hear what she said to him, because she was careful for the Disciplines of the Wars.

GLYN JONES

PARK

The tiny cream-bricked lighthouse on the hill
Glitters seeing all and this. The island grass
Is silent and pale green, the high dry tide
Deep blue-wood water, smooth and shadowless,
Smooth to the white upright collar of the cliff.
One tealeaf swimmer swims that dusty sea.
Radiant and woollen gold, the sun sees too
The tilted gold-browed moon bent on the little park
Whose paths are heaped with snow, or burntwood black.
Over the velvet railings of the pond
A white-edged hunchback feeds a swan with cake.
The fancy bridge has bamboo legs, combs back
The rivers long blue hair; and on its hump a boy
Bald-headed, wearing lemon boots, leans back
Flying the fish-kite, while his Jessie sits
On gaudy grass to touch the raisin tree.
Pass, doves, and pass you coal-flanked elephant
Jessie's tall corn-coloured tree,
Make with your crimson satan-satin sash
Towards the glittering lighthouse, where its glass
Flashes like crossed scissors in the sun.

ESYLLT

As he climbs down our hill, my kestrel rises,
Steering in silence up from five empty fields,
A smooth sun brushed brown across his shoulders,
Floating in wide circles, his warm wings stiff.
Their shadows cut; in new soft orange hunting boots
My lover crashes through the snapping bracken.

The still gorse-hissing hill burns, brags gold broom's
Outcropping quartz; each touched bush spills dew.
Strangely last moment's parting was never sad,
Than this intense white silver snail calligraphy
Scrawled here in the sun across these stones.

Why have I often wanted to cry out
More against his going when he has left my flesh
Only for the night? When he has gone out
Hot from my mother's kitchen, and my combs
Were on the table under the lamp, and the wind
Was banging the doors of the shed in the yard.

GULL

Not tiring round the shores his rigid shadow, prompt
Beneath the landing webs that touch the sand,
Not kiting over-white against torn winds,
Milkily wheeling on brim-tilt wings, or heaping up
Burnt breeze behind, with cutting air in ovals,
The long slant cornering, his steep-sloped pointed wings
Speed-canted speed-heeled over, leaned like skidding wheels.

But
Behind the cape day's great sun hits the sea;
Rain greys two blue bays; his flesh his plumes
Flame-flushed, the burning gull flees bearing fast
Fire flashed out, launched across the flooded east;
Blush-feathered, frocked, above the grey-bled sea
He bears my beating heart with rosy webs,
That fire-bird, the flame-silked through the grieving sea-rain,
    swift
On hot flushed petal-flesh his flashing wings.

BEACH

Hears the heavy rising hay
  Dry-throat down his blade of land;
Hears the dim wind strum, strum,
  Behind the blushing bony wing,
Hears it from that sand-struck wreck
  That black smooth spoonful of sand.
Gazes up the bare beach, sees
  Pass again that slow bored gull,
The broken daisy-chain of rain.
  Grey, razor-fine horizon cuts
Far beyond the deckless hull;
  Kissed, the sunset mouthroof-red,
The golden half-moon Gwil's hung glove;
  Kissed Gwil on the harelip twice,
Gwil, my love, my love.

SANDE

Sande's crucifix, that criss-cross star;
The risking saint, naked and upright on
His crop of hills, prays up against the dark.
The winds pluck off his skidding flesh like leaves,
His red remainder bone-shrub chants, that tick-
Tack thicket of his upright skeleton
Reissues praises from a mouth of bone,
And through the black lantern-holes of both his eyes
His holy bones can see his morning star.
The melted lightning yellows on his head,
His zigzag bones are bedstraws on his rocks;
Scattered he prays and sees his pulsing star.

ALAN PRYCE JONES

SAID THE CAPTAIN

I am sick of war, said the captain;
I never liked that kind of thing.
Give me my black Mercury on the card-table
And my slanting walks in the sun.
Give me peace, said the captain.
Somewhere a dusty light between the bays
Falls on Plato and a sweet biscuit
While I am groaned upon.
Keep your whole, said the captain,
Your plumed courage and outspread wing.
Make plans, execute, be able;
Leave me the bare begun,
The glimpsed, the fraction, said the captain;
They shall deserve my holidays.
These dear scantlings of mine won't fit,
He said, into a confident One.
As for your purposes and glories
Do with them what you please;
I have the whole country in my nostrils
And all the past under my eye.
I like brinks, said the captain,
And I know nothing about victories;
But, ah, I know how morning
Strikes the warm pane and the thudding bee.

S. G. LEONARD

MORON

Fish;
Nor art in this:
Caribou and cow are wed.
Only a wrinkled cherub at a fun-fair
In saxophone-diapason stumbled abed.
Sing, anger, sing
Or roll a-metric
To a diatribe of the greased sniveller.

Fish;
Nor friend in this.
Call a cuckoo by its name.
To have heard a groan (the smile
Deceived my steps) had saved a lane
Unpeacocked
And be-puddled
That spun the ooze within a soul.

THE MISTRESS

Her printed breath should be a flower
Frozen in a mirror that wants not words
To tell astonishment. But I am old
And visit her as winds do winds, to fight her face,
Watch scowling hair packed over that white wound
And give my love and all my love's great grief
To hands of air, grey lips, eyes of dumb stone,
Some bliss of Hell, Hell's shocking naught, for her
Ever quietly screaming.

She sends me the true treaty, printed breath
With poison in a kiss; reveals bright bodies
Turned to dark where once the dazzled thunder
Barked through my brain and built up views
While wonder trod the clouds. Sometimes
I plucked a hill from a socket of smoke
And fashioned it with fingers to a toy
For this spoilt child who bragged and banged
False praise as a club on the brittle head
Knocking its begetter with noisy blood.
But yet in this my love's rude speech
There dwells a statue that must rise to breathe,
Prance, vapourlike, on the revolving street,
Expand and blind with beauty.
As long as thunder prompts and lightnings rock
She will demand, stab underfoot and brawl,
Break every vow, and in the trysting winds
Keep lovers' watch till grief grows big with child
And if she ask I'll give and will not share;
Love's portion is to please and be displeased.

ALBAN A. LEVY

OUT OF A DUST . . .

Out of a dust, I came, bewildered,
Stretching uncertain fingers to the light.
Out of a dust, obscurely lingered
The half dim memories of the birth night.
Into the cradle wood, made mother
The wildest greeting for the elder son,
Into the world the doubting brother
Out of the dust and shapeless shadow run.

When the warm hearth clicks with the weather,
As surely all our youthful fabrics must
Come by the hangman's cart together,
Softly the slow footfall treads in the dust.
Calloo, the wind cries, raining, raining,
And the sky moves windward with the season.
Cry wind—calloo, complain, complaining
The broken parapet with no reason.

ALUN LEWIS

THE SENTRY

I have begun to die.
For now at last I know
That there is no escape
From Night. Not any dream
Nor breathless images nor sleep
Touch my bat's-eyes. I hang
Leathery-arid from the hidden roof
Of Night; and sleeplessly
I watch within sleep's province.
I have left
The lovely bodies of the boy and girl
Deep in each other's placid arms,
And I have left
The beautiful lanes of sleep
That barefoot lovers follow to this last
Cold shore of thought I guard.
I have begun to die
And the guns' implacable silence
Is my black interim, my youth and age,
In the flower of Fury, the folded poppy,
NIGHT.

RIVER RHONDDA

By broken shafts the greasy river
Rhondda drops her veils of scum
On dirty rocks to mark the ancient
Degraded union of stone and water.

By banks of ashes unwashed colliers
Gamble for luck the pavements hide:
Kids float tins down noisy rapids:
Coaldust rings the scruffy willows:
Circe is a drab.

She gives men what they know.
Daily to her pitch-black shaft
She sucks husbands from their sleep;
And for her profit takes their hands and eyes.

But the fat flabby-breasted wives
Have grown accustomed to her ways.
They scrub, make tea, peel the potatoes—

Without counting the days.

TO EDWARD THOMAS

(On visiting the memorial stone above Steep.)

I

On the way up from Steep I met some children
Filling a pram with brushwood; higher still,
Beside Steep church, an old man pointed out
A small white stone upon a flinty spur
Projecting from the high autumnal woods. . . .
I doubt if much has changed since you came here
On your last leave; except the stone; it bears
Your name and trade: 'To Edward Thomas, Poet.'

II

Climbing the steep path through the copse I knew
My cares weighed heavily as yours, my gift
Much less, my hope
No more than yours.
And like you I felt sensitive and somehow apart,
Lonely and exalted with the friendship of the wind
And the silent afternoon enfolding
The dangerous future and the smile.

III

I sat and watched the dusky berried ridge
Of yew trees, deepened by oblique dark shafts,
Throw back the flame of red and gold and russet
That leapt from beech and ash to birch and chestnut
Along the downward arc of the hill's shoulder,
And sunlight streaming from the wind-blown branches
Softly explore the distant wooded acres
And plotted tilth, and with discerning fingers
Touch the white farmsteads one by one with lightness
Until it reached the Downs, whose soft green pastures
Went slanting sea- and sky-wards to the edge
Where sight surrenders and the mind alone
Can find the sheep's tracks and the grazing.
And for that moment life appeared
As lovely as the view I gazed upon.

IV

Later, a whole day later, I remembered
This war and yours and your weary
Circle of failure and your striving
To make articulate the groping voices
Of snow and rain and dripping branches
And love that ailing in itself cried out

About the straggling eaves and ringed the candle
With shadows slouching round your buried head;
And in the waiting room there was no ease
For you, or Helen, or those small perplexed
Children of yours who only wished to please. . . .

V

Divining this, I knew the voice that called you
Was soft and neutral as the sky's
Arc or the grey horizon, stronger
Than Night's immediate grasp, the limbs of mercy
Oblivious as the blood, and growing sharper,
More urgent as all else dissolved away—
Projected books, half-thoughts, the children's birthdays
And wedding anniversaries as cold
As dates in history—the dream
Emerging from the fact, and farther still,
The fact beyond that dream,
The endless rides of stormy-branchéd dark
Whose fibres are a thread within the hand—
Till suddenly, at Arras, you possessed that hinted land.

THE DEFEATED: FOR WALES

'Sooner will his blood be spent than he go to the wedding feast.
No hatred shall there be between thee and me; better will I do
thee, to praise thee in song.' (*A Welsh Poem—seventh–ninth
century.*)

Our courage is an old legend.
We left the fields of our fathers.
Fate was our foeman.

We held the world in our fingers
And threw it like a farthing
That needed no keeping.

More love was there never
By Euphrates and Tigris
Than in our proud country.

Love was our talisman.
We were blinded in battle
By the weeping of women.

Bled white are our wounds,
Wounds writhing with worms;
All spilt the quick seed. . . .

Oh! dark are we whose greed for life
Was a green slash in our eyes
And in our darkness we are wise,

Forgetting honour, valour, fame,
In this darkness whence we came.

THE MOUNTAIN OVER ABERDARE

From this high quarried ledge I see
The place for which the Quakers once
Collected clothes, my fathers' home,
Our stubborn bankrupt village sprawled
In jaded dusk beneath its nameless hills;
The drab streets strung across the cwm,
Derelict workings, tips of slag
The gospellers and gamblers use
And children scrutting for the coal
That winter dole cannot purvey;
Allotments where the collier digs
While engines hack the coal within his brain;
Grey Hebron in a rigid cramp,

White cheap-jack cinema, the church
Stretched like a sow beside the stream;
And mourners in their Sunday best
Holding a tiny funeral, singing hymns
That drift insidious as the rain
Which rises from the steaming fields
And swathes about the skyline crags
Till all the upland gorse is drenched
And all the creaking mountain gates
Drip brittle tears of crystal peace;
And in a curtained parlour women hug
Huge grief, and anger against God.

But now the dusk, more charitable than Quakers,
Veils the cracked cottages with drifting may
And rubs the hard day off the slate.
The colliers squatting on the ashtip
Listen to one who holds them still with tales,
While that white frock that floats down the dark alley
Looks just like Christ; and in the lane
The clink of coins among the gamblers
Suggests the thirty pieces of silver.

I watch the clouded years
Rune the rough foreheads of these moody hills,
This wet evening, in a lost age.

THE SOLDIER
I

I within me holding
Turbulence and Time—
Volcanic fires deep beneath the glacier—
Feel the dark cancer in my vitals
Of impotent impatience grope its way
Through daze and dream to throat and fingers
To find its climax of disaster.

The sunlight breaks its glittering wings
Imprisoned in the Hall of Mirrors;
Nightmare rides upon the headlines;
While Summer leaves her green reflective woods
And flashes momently on peaks of madness.
But leisurely my fellow soldiers stroll among the trees.
The cheapest dance song utters all they feel.

II

Now as a lover would
Kiss while walking
I in the beech copse
By the chalk-pit
Stand and marvel
At the finches'
Identical beauty
Heraldic markings
Power of wings
To flicker and blossom
On branches of song.

Say that they lust
And squabble and die
Say their glancing copulation
Poised flutter on a twig
Ignores the holy mystery
Of boy and girl
Together timelessly.

III

Yet still
I who am agonized by thought
And war and love
Grow calm again
With watching

The flash and play of finches
Who are as beautiful
And as indifferent to me
As England is, this Spring morning.

MID-WINTER

Old Dafydd, eyes like bloodhound's red with age,
Told me in passing, dropping his brushwood to say,
'The waves freeze as they fall. It is indeed
Funny to hear that silence, 'tis indeed!'
And blew upon his blue and broken nails
And rubbed his mittened hands and shouldered up
The ice and earth encrusted twigs of beech
And said 'Good night. And mind in this cold spell
You do not loiter,' and then lumbered on.

I took the path to the sea along the ruts
Whose crystals cracked and crunched beneath my boots.
The frost-bound mountains, tuned like tightened strings,
Quivered beneath the hawk's exalted dream.
The disused quarry, red with peat and iron,
Suspended frozen stalactites of moss.
The briars' vernal thrust
Writhed vainly in the icewomb of the soil,
And all the meadows screamed through sharp green tongues
Dumbly and blacklipped stretched upon the rack,
For the loosening laughter of rain and the runnels' race.
And I like the grass cried out
In the ice of your absence clutched
For the sun in the sunken night,
For a proof of your escape,
For your coming home.

And when I came to the shore I felt you pull
My heart as the passionate wave
Answered the moontug, leaped, and in high poise
Tense in a timeless curve contained itself,
Then broke, ah broke, and shattered and seethed all white
Up the green and purple pebble beach—the reach
Of desire that rushes white from the swirl of pain.
So my heart leaped high and ached for your coming again
As the earth for the longed-for, long awaited
Blessing of the rain.

At last the benediction, the soft release,
The bending of grass, the dripping from moss and leaf,
When I heard the fall of your sandal on the sand
And I felt your body breathing by my side,
When my heart like a grove of birds sang back again
Your coming, your home-returning, farer-forth,
To my charred and ashen hearth whose heap of sticks
Your nostril's breath rekindles, Cytherea,
Who stand so silent, hesitant, engrossed.
O warm your aching hands
At my soul's reviving flame,
And tell me, if you choose,
Of your troubled voyaging down
Through the chasms of time and pain,
Of the stress of the rocks on your soul,
And your soul's escape.

But your puckered forehead and distracted eyes
Tell of a madness too intense for word
Or kiss or loving pity to dispel.
Yet, having come to me,
Lie quietly, beloved in my arms;
Let us forget
In the warmth of the flesh the dry and hidden bone,
In the curve of the wave its shattering on the stone,

And sleep within my breathing, sweetheart, sleep,
While the wood smoke curls through Dafydd's leaking thatch
And the river runs again with gladness to the sea.

ROLAND MATHIAS

BALLOON OVER THE RHONDDA

We had gone down to Tabor, to the door
My corduroy a green
Tug at the ministerial spleen, a tweak
At the white scarf-knot, peak in pocket seen
Capping the diaconate,
In time to scalp the noise
And scamper made by boys, evacuees
With paper aeroplanes the teasing wind
Forced down behind the chapel rails.
Sighs from the big seat
Came barely out
Above the scrabble of the eager boots
Climbing the gate
        for paperweight . . .

The tease was bold that night,
Suborns of bigger men had gone adrift:
The little clusters in the street
Sent eyes up to the south
And feet were still:

A silver elephant with wings
Came curveting and lolloping
With a one-sided smile.
He turned and chortled, lay down on his back
And laughed, helpless and rolling.

Up from the east came the stern searing of
The pursuit wasp,
In the ballooning laughter poured
First secondsworth of venom and a silence,
Then the wide curve of steady preparation
And seconds more.
The ears fell back
And all the laughter wasted:
Falling a thousand feet the narrow hide
Pine end hung on
In dumb deflation.
Three other Spitfires flew a higher course
Poured in their angled heat
And passed.
Dying in sullenness
The skin a sagging five miles off
Caught of the glory a few sunset rays
Clung to its thousand feet and stooped
Up to the valley head:
Obstinate blob upon the sky
Bleak with attendant stings
It passed behind the housetops
Uncomprehending and absurd.

'Duw, if that Whitley'd hit 'er
She'd 'a shifted' and the remark
Gave the cloth cap an air.
Speculation soon and hands
Went back in pockets
And the whole street on heels again.

Out of the gateway old Arafna John
Signalman's line of red gone thin
Below the waist in black
Came with the deacons to attack their caps
Cordon their eyes perhaps at green and gawk.

'Whose son is this?' and talk apace
Of the pregethwr . . . Green in the eyes again
And no grace in the pause
(The sunset passed behind the mine) . . .
O could the slow vine be husbanded
The branch sweeping the grass?
Better the doubt than diction
Thinking John he said
'I hope you'll set the world to rights, my son'
And plodded on.
Under the sky they were the dumb who nodded.

HUW MENAI

IN THE VALE OF GLAMORGAN

Bird-men, the devil's alloy in their metal,
  Go roaring Southward while a throstle sings;
Above, then below the clouds—wonder of wonders!
  The sunset's beauty flashing on their wings,

And I, with humble sparrows in the cornfield,
  Know less of exultation than of pain
For thinking that these miracles of conquest
  May not come home again!

CWM FARM NEAR CAPEL CURIG

Some cool medieval calm hath settled here
  On this lone farmstead, wherein humble folk
  Still speak the tongue that Owain Glyndwr spoke.
And worship in it, too, the God they fear.
For to these perilous Ways, where rocks rise sheer,

Their kinsmen came to curse the tyrant yoke;
And here the proud invader's heart was broke
By brave and stubborn men year after year.
Unconquerable still! here birds but know
  The Cymric speech; the very mountains brood
O'er consonants that, rugged streamlets, flow
  Into deep vowel lakes . . . and by this wood,
  Where Prince Llywelyn might himself have stood,
Forget-me-nots in wild profusion grow!

THE OLD PEASANT IN THE BILLIARD SALOON

Stretched out full length, his eighty years too ripe
  For upright posture, on the bench each day
Sleeping aloud, or tugging at his pipe,
  Or one eye open on the billiard play.
A sufferer from old age too wise for tears!
  And does he see, in that smoke-ridden place,
Th' Almighty Cueist sending the different spheres
  Upon their business spinning through all space?
Or does it make for a more homely scene,
  With him a lusty youth in Somerset
Bringing the cattle home through fields of green?
  Muttering of something that he has not met!
  Muttering to himself, his later sense
  Having found none worthier of his confidence!

BACK IN THE RETURN

Where shall the eyes a darkness find
That is a menace to the mind
Save in the coal mine, where one's lamp
Is smothered oft by afterdamp?
Down there is found the deepest gloom,
Where Night is rotting in her tomb:

It is a being, something fraught
With evil, clutching at man's throat.
And O! the stillness underground!
Oppressive silence, ne'er a sound,
Save for a dribble here, and there,
A gas-pop, or a gust of air,
When idle are the wheels, and one
Sits down to listen, all alone;
When one will welcome, with surprise
The unmelodious squeaks of mice;
From Baltic beetles gladly take,
And Jaspers, what small sounds they make—
To face it one must needs be brave
This silence of an old world's grave!
But when full work is on, the air
Does a more homely garment wear,
When sometimes, floating on the foul,
Comes 'Jesu Lover of my Soul',
Between spat Baccy Juice and smut,
From hewers squatting in the 'cut';
Or, coming from more distant stalls,
The rhythmic tap of mandril falls
Upon the ear till one would swear
The pulse of *Earth* was beating there.

Back in the foul Return
Where bodies of men burn
Out, out before their time,
Where dead is the sublime,
And murdered is the soul
To keep the brute alive;
Where lust is in control,
Still young the sensitive
Must die, still young—
His songs unsung!

The mine is no romantic place—
It stinks of Hell from sump to 'face';
A honeycomb of headings, stalls,
Airways, drifts, and rubbish walls.
Intake fresh, and foul Return,
Which lighted once becomes an urn
For human ashes!

'A beershop meeting! First a wink,
A smutty yarn, a leer, a drink,
Another drink, and then another. . . .'
To smother self-respect, to smother
The latent grace in womanhood,
The latent grace that long withstood
The onslaught of the Evil One,—
Too late! the dirty work is done!
A ribald song, some further dope
To grease again the downward slope,
One little push, the devil begs,
And then—the bottom, and the dregs! . . .

'A beershop meeting! I've no name;
From out the guts of Chance I came
To shock the goody-goody lot
Who snivel o'er the devil's pot;
Who make from out the devil's wash
An appetizing pulpit hash;
A beershop meeting! I've no name;
A child of sin, a child of shame,
Conceived among the slush and slime
And born to fester into crime
Had I not caught some luck in time
And struck against the sucking in
Of milk that was three parts of gin.
The milk flew up to mother's head,
And, in her tantrums, she fell dead.

And so I was, a babe, set free
To cut my teeth in Charity;
To bite an artificial teat,
To suck my fists, to find my feet
Implanted firmly on the Rates,
The bogey-bo of Christian States;
A nuisance, nameless brat, unwanted!
Yet through it all for life I panted,
For life, for life to tell the Fates
They had no right to burden Rates.

'I grew to corduroy, and clogs;
I grew a skill for cutting logs;
I grew to bite the Labour Master
Who kicked me for not cutting faster,
To butt Tramp Major in the belly
For trying a cure on me with skilly;
I grew to break my share of stones;
I grew a hatred in my bones;
And as one booked to bend my spine
I left the Workhouse for the mine.'

EXTRACT FROM 'BACK IN THE RETURN'

'Hungry, and penniless, an Out-of-Work,
  Who once the poise of dignity knew well,
No longer now a stranger to the stoop
  That would the heartbreak tell.
Trudging the City streets, my wondering eyes
  Gay Lords and Ladies, in their cars pursue,
Who fly from their monotony of good times
  To seek sensations new—
On my pale face, in the agony of my mood,
  My miner's scars standing like clots of blood!

'Amazed, I watched the rushing human river,
  As Night stooped down to light the shops and cars
Then, on the cold sarcophagus of For Ever,
  Inscribe her challenging hieroglyphs of stars.
And when I closed mine eyes, to be alone,
  I heard, deep down within that mass of souls,
A troubled wind that moaned in unison
  With the doleful litany of sulking owls,
For all the pleasure-hunting, all its air
  Of knowing Joy. And thought my misery:
If only Christ was on point-duty there
  To regulate the traffic, one would see
In the great scab called Piccadilly less
  The supreme sign of national rottenness.'

THE STARS LOOK DOWN

The stars look down and who shall stand
  And say they come from Mercy's hand,
That they reflect in their clear skies
  The glow from every-pitying eyes.

The stars look down as on we go
  Poor mortals tossed 'tween weal and woe
Each with a lonely soul in keep
  Each with a wealth of tears to weep.

The stars look down as through the night
  We waste our precious mutual light
In conflict till we reach the gate
  To keep our final tryst with Fate!

STALINGRAD

May it for ever live to be
The blood-soaked symbol of the Free
Against whose walls of pride and pain
The might of Evil stormed in vain.

May it, too, stand a beacon light
To help us through the after night
Make a New World in a brave mould
Out of the rubble of the Old!

THE INEXORABLE

Bitterly they fought, for that planet room,
    Darkness their ally, where they could not see
Good in each other for a hatred, blind,
    Battling for breath, *hitting* from memory.
And how one grieved to think their damaged hands
    Needed more shattering ere they could hope to win
The Power to raise the curtain on their gloom
    And let the healing light of heaven come in!

B. J. MORSE

EVENTUAL BIRTH OF THOUGHT

(For Rosemary Johnson)

My communioned figment impales the moon
and blazons golden lightbeams of the noon
on each imperilled respite of my day
when stricken quivers whir spheres in my way:

the darkening shelter of eternity
meteors on through voids to spinning clod,
and grandeured flashes of immensity
turn up their headlights on a wakening God:—

tremulous the fane of sir-reverend sirs
that satellited round the sod-dark blurs
of unaverted chance that erstwhile wrought
in this estranging way the birth of thought.

JOHN PRICHARD

POEM

Is there virtue in the sweet medium?
Is moderation wisdom and excess folly?
Like the swung pendulum, mean or extremity
May be the attained, the come-to-rest of all.

How subdivide the treasons of the heart
To the willed goal; gear down fancy with the cogs
Of rule and hit it off with grey and red?
How strike a balance with the head and heart?

Age plods with lead leg the old road
While hogging Youth fevers and scorches the new track.
How hotfoot it with the shanks of Age in Youth's
Quick shortcuts? How graft the weathered head
With the unshut heart, leaving the essence free?
And which reaches, the old road in the ruck?

EASTER POEM

A thunder and whirlwind pluck out the eyestone.
He humbles out, not lily from the grave,
But ash-touching cerements shedding green meteors
Of glowworms from His shoulders and His star-bound head;
Albino from the nest of bats
With furry toadstools at His ears.

The doubting poke with their practical fingers
And the fishflesh crumbles through the skin.
The relicked bones are polished in museums;
A plate-passing piety communions in Christendom.
The censer-swung continents kneel in prayer
But cannot camouflage denial, the tar and feathers.

He smells His dead
He hears the wind a tattler of lies
Sees the summer crops shall be monuments of evil
And the days' suns are father to sin
And all His bright birds carry poison for His mouth
He sees them who stitched Him to the Cross.

This for His torrent tears and grief
This for the valleys of His blood
This for the vinegar and the crown of thorns
This for His Passion
Death for death
And this is His kingdom.

A thunder bids Him not loiter in the world
Weeping-sad. The waters of the earth
Have shaped His wind-worn cheek. The snows that bite
His flesh, the cracking frosts and God's enduring
Weathers now have made ruin of Him.

His bones of stone and His moss flesh have
Bleached skin and fungus hair where worms go
And dull as clouds are His moon's eyes
And the stars of His weevilled eyes put out.

He turns to the catacomb
And goes down from the sun,
Two bloody gems carbuncled in his palms.

POEM

When birds and brittle leaves come down
When trees and grass freeze out their blood
And fishes die in floods of rain,
This is the time for Death.
A mouse is spiked on blades of grass
A sparrow swings from the gibbet of a twig.
This is the time I die
When a tablet of blood, the seas dissolve the sun
And barren nests are cups to catch the rain.

When gathered leaves and rags of weed
When trees decay like teeth and hair,
Fallen, broadcast in winter's care,
How at my head and house winds battle
And the perilous seed drops in me.
Tears are like rivulets in snow
Threatening the personal landscape.

When roar the rivers rush through my country's throat
It is torrents from a severed artery.
Blood finds a way to the sea
The blood from cemeteries
The blood from dead within me
The black blood from within me.

Nature is a token from the dead,
This dew how sweet and fresh
The sweat of the dead.
Death's fertile, more than life.
A tree grows from the restless loins
Flowers from the head
Threading patterns through bones and brains
With bloom of flesh on petals and leaves
To charm the world with images of Death.

THE GREEN NAVIES

*('O Christ! to think of the green navies and the green-
skulled crews.'*—HERMAN MELVILLE.)

By Capricorn seas and typhoon
Or stove hatch death sands their eyes
With a quick salt end,
A watch below in the sea-bed schools.
Only Mother Carey's chickens
See them go; squawk and scavenge.

Davy Jones's crews: in two tides
A squid has their blood and magpie
Fish have cached their jewel eyes;
Jumbos rub their flanks away;
A crab hermits in the empty skull
And big-sea brooms polish their ribs.

Their souls inhabit rats; their flesh
Fell in a hundred ports; speech
Was broadcast in lost winds.
Only a seaman moonraking over
The wall, pipes the green navies;
Can see a coral cross of bones.

POEM

In fear of death do not neglect small bounty
Which costs but life; gratitude to the hands which
Scattered free favours, gemmed the trees
With cluster buds that bubble in April flocks
And the green hosts of Spring
And the invisible beak that preens,
The breath that tinkers them.

Acid rain which spots the hand and skull
Burns terror in the skin. The stung cheek
Learns humility from the brand of winds.

Fear the fine season's shoot
And the veteran, crooked with a load of years;
Fear the seas run booming in the bay
And the force that furls the sea,
Drags the trundling cloud in a tumbled sky.
And fear the hands that lit the sun.

Fear, O fear the million mouths
That stir but do not speak
Of charity or any comfort
Teach save life in death,
In fear of which do not despise small bounty.

SWANSEA BAY

Here would seem a mastery of time
And sufferance of that academic death.
Here delivered by grace of water, conspiracy
Of wind and moon are foreigners commuted
For a tide's abidance to this instant slate,
Stranded on the littoral; shells without tenant,

A ruffled, rare-lidded gull in shroud of oil
And a dog snarling with rib and tooth
In a lethal embrace of needy stones.

The static, shipless sea of false waves
Poised and propped beyond the claybeds, the blind
Lighthouse, the map sun set in a barren
Sky, a painted flat, and these starched gravegrooms
Scaring like laid by the wayside coffins and all
The hushed, unweathered beach, still and spent,
Irreducible as its sandgrains, compose
A breath-holding scene, a daylight exhumation,
Life's pattern caught and built in a moment's pose.

Extremity is nearest to eternity.
This pedestalled world behind a dike of time
And this petrified emotion snapped
In the flat, heraldic seascape now tell
Life in tableau, show time in statuary.

GORONWY REES

THE LANDSCAPE FADING

The landscape fading dims my eyes
And shows what mind has built within,
Absence struck, so rock and stream
Are signs that sorrow must begin.

Golden sands, the faithful sea
We took for joy and love: but faithless
Inconstant they remain to taunt the heart
Blind to its own creativeness.

Parting is winter that denudes our trees,
Winging birds southward with fall of leaf,
And sours affections that by presence lived
Which absence in its need abstracts to grief.

THE SEASONS' FOOL

The heartbreak fall of sound recurs
Incessant, change gives up its prey
And sets the peasant prisoner free:
Body with fatal mind concurs,
When living sloughs its death and birth,
In autumn to protect the trees
And winter keeps the snow away;
Intolerant passion cannot agree
To seasonal changes in the earth.

But since first love has been betrayed
And the body of timeless joy
The limbs that seemed to touch the soul,
For my new lover now afraid,
In terror of ghost and faded leaf,
I wonder how I may destroy
The seasons that turn me into fool
Who find old beauties come to grief.

Yet though I take my body up
That intellect has left for dead
Foredoomed to time and tide of sense,
And make it free of its mishap,
I know she is the seasons' child
With young corn in its earthy bed
And greenness of the spring's pretence
And harvest creatures of the wild.

I would not wish her otherwise:
To bring her to this lonely place
Where I escape captivity
Must make her lose her sensual ties.
This mind that integrates my walls
Is part of earth that gives her grace
But harsh voiced with world's enmity
Against my bleak and broken halls.

KEIDRYCH RHYS

EPHEMERAE FOR BRUSKA

Stories of many slants, gods of sea and sky
Courted by whispers spotted in the wind
Where deepset eyes, still heroes, caught still older legend:
Many, as you know, long haunt lounge through guest house
      wind.

These, without apparent purpose; what the postcards say
Of their pictured leap over stone
She who taught a bird the word (a fly in my eye)
Or of Arthur's hound hunting boar and sow
Is rum. Though now dawn spirits squint at water's dawn stone.

Elsewhere the others were led astray on the mountain
According to plan; the scribble was only mountain—
A formula for a curse; and over the dwarf's grave
Stood the brindled mastiff, the dog guarding the cave.

Mound, well, hearth, then crossed; nodded the physicians,
Noted the lidded couple beside the misty lake
On their way to Woolworths; here a custom crossed; passed
The child-eating hag with a sprig of hazel; oh great yes great!

Except for mistaking the rowan in the cwm for apple tree
The marches stirred for our three breasted lover, also hill.
True this resembled other world witchcraft or banknotes; still
The florid were cured by yarn; the needy set free to marts.
And we learnt madness by degree and ate our fathers' hearts.

DURING LAMBING SEASON

Side by side let elder sheep roll over on spring earth
huts are dry and full in Talley, china blue eyes write signs of
    birth.
Here's work for boys in long corduroys from Mothvey to
    Goldengrove
all through that summer's rogue Ryland ram's brief noncon-
    formist love!
Oh the young devils are tough with bleeding navels lean on
    ground;
by elements torn, brown hairstuff licked, prayer suck, born
    worth a £.
Wander off like postman, sex by chapel ballot to save funeral
    expense
Still no need to ridicule Sabbath morning pack out of existence.
Up on a ditch one inhales fag's smoke on account of hand closed
    flesh,
their ears are made of a god's carpet, cut out; a penknife mesh;
too weak you say, well kitchen fire, whisky in a silver spoon,
    ma's ah!
false baba sentiment! these parents wear no bells; but the same
    happens baa baa;
low-bellied, hedge-breakers, man's bloody marvel, organized on
    purple hill:
do it with an arm in a sling; drown to a rook's rainy stare; die
    of woolball.

RIVER SAWDDE

When I step thimble heeled at an end of day
Sound of water Sawdde water pricks my ear,
A spreading dynamo sheer over all stone
Except for the round ribbed ones to wash it by.

Never trunk of tree on a sunken 'twmpath'
Met man or bill or hedging glove as I was there,
No smell no taste no speaking cold by people with a bell
In the finished disc of moon could but resemble

The next line open in wind tremble, heart whole being
Up the hillside moving as if telltale fingers
Were uncoffined at some thread; a mascot falls in love.

What it is to have water running near one's own house
With eels in it—alone—real—a one-syllabled water language.
Those town fellows have borrowed beetles in their shoes!

SHEEP

Limp in lambing weather
Sheep curve over shining snow
As collies command
And worry on the slow

Huddled in larch hurdles
Branded by index ear
Play for dog-trials
Again they wait in fear

Rinsed in mountain torrent
Held to shearing machine
Next disinfectant
Poking through of bone

110

Bane of braking motorist
Bound for peasant cottage
They winter twenty miles away
Beyond a Cardigan village

Behind—Cheviots of early start
Bleating of loaded truck
Sharp bids at Lampeter mart
And the smile of a butcher's cheque

POEM FOR A NEIGHBOUR

In the sea-marsh where I carve the harsh shallows
On the turfed rock rise a shock of willows
Stockdoves, fireflies, sea-gulls, bats from the hollows.

In the sea-marsh where outlaws starve with my Molly
On open knoll scrolls of black alder sea-holly
Instead of the screech-owl's extravagant folly.

In the sea-marsh where the buzz-hawk's talk is drover
On sea-pulses, rag-tag, lurking circles, clover
Love-sick flicks light the nightmares of our half-drunk lover.

In the sea-marsh now springtime graves new paved with dew
On Ovid's buckler a trysting moon to Tresaith grew,
Winnowed the heathcocks, magpies, cranes, sea-eagles flew.

INTERLUDE

Simply I would sing for the time being
Of the wayward hills I must make my feeling.
The rickety bicycle, the language of birds
Caught fishing up the church street for preaching words,

111

The deacon hawking swedes, the gyppos clapping, on
Their way to vans over common's crushed sandstone
And the milk stands so handy to sit upon!
The roadmen laying pipes of local cement
The Italian's chip shop and the village comment;
'No reserve; all they know on the tip of their tongue'.
That educated tramp from the lodging house league.

The lady, the lake, both sleeping, the cattle
Called back through stories, bells silent, a deep down rattle:
Comics, rivers well-named, dense gorse floodlights valley's
Gurgling. Grief in a mailbag, drama on trolleys.
Less and less shoeing for smith, farming's polite dying,
'Messiah' in the chapel—but a warning, gulls crying
Up at Easter miners off the race's soothing colour.
Oh simply simply I sing down the masterly contour.

TRAGIC GUILT

No. I'm not an Englishman with a partisan religion.
My roots lie in another region,
Though ranged alongside yours.

Here I sense your stubbornness and your cohesion
And can even feel pride in your recent decision
That anger reassures.

I know no love for disembodied principles, improbable tales.
The strength of the common man was always the strength of
        Wales,
Unashamed of her race.

May this be also England's rôle to bring to birth.
May she draw opposite new powers from the earth.
Huge Shakespeare has his place.

I have felt in my bones comradeship and pity,
I have seen wonders in an open door blitz city.

Amid tremendous history, new pity.

YOUTH

I try to remember the things
At home that mean Wales but typical
Isn't translated across
The Channel: I try to create,
Doors grow into masts, love losses
In the village wood, but boyhood's
Fear fled into the pale skeleton
Of the dark mountain, into
The bilingual valley filled
Through a sail-hole of my drying
Feelings. But I try. Lightning
Is different in Wales.

LYNETTE ROBERTS

TO THE PRIEST OF THE MIDDLES

(*concerning the New Order*)

If there is to be freedom of mind and face,
If there is to be mind of different weight,
Then there can be no equality of race,
Neither of mind nor face; for the late
Mind might want what a quick mind could ban.

To give face and freedom to mass production
And cramp our mind to the dead-piece, can
Hardly mature equality of race, station
The heart socially. It would merely provoke
Late mind to mud and quick mind to silver:
Hard 'middles' is the answer: thus to invoke
I am content to stay a cottage harbinger
Content to express the fury of a kind
At this attack on the precincts of a mind.

EXTRACT FROM 'A HEROIC POEM'

We must uprise O my people. Though
Secretly trenched in sorrel, we must
Upshine, outshine the day's sun: and day
Intensified by the falling haggard
Of rain shall curve our smile with straw.

Bring plimsole plover to the tensile sand
And with cuprite crest and petulant feet
Distil our notes into febrile weeds
Crisply starched at the water-rail of tides.
On gault and greensand a gramophone stands:

In zebeline stripes strike out the pilotless
Age: from saxophone towns brass out the dead:
Disinter futility, that we entombing men
Might bridle our runaway hearts.
On tamarisk, on seafield pools shivering

With water-cats, ring out the square slate notes.
Shape the birdbox trees with neumes. Wind sound
Singular into cool and simple corners,
Round pale bittern grass, and all unseen
Unknown places of sheltered rubble

Where whimbrels, redshanks, dunlins ripple
For the wing of living. Under tin of earth,
And wooden boles where owls break music:
From this killing world against Humanity,
Uprise against, outshine the day's sun.

LAMENTATION

To the village of lace and stone
Came strangers. I was one of these
Always observant and slightly obscure.
I roamed the hills of bird and bone
Rescuing bees from under the storm:
Five hills rocked and four homes fell
The day I remember the raid so well.
Eyes shone like cups chipped and stiff
The living bled, the dead lay in their grief
Cows, sheep, horses, all had got struck
Black as bird wounds, red as wild duck:

DEAD as icebone breaking the hedge.
DEAD as soil failing of good heart.
DEAD as trees quivering with shock
At the hot death from the plane.

O the cold loss of cattle
With their lovely big eyes.
The emptiness of sheds,
The rick stacked high.
The breast of the hills
Will soon turn grey
As the dogs that grieve
And I that fetched them in:
For the good gates are closed
In the yard down our way.

But my loss! My loss is greater
Than Rosie's of Chapel House Farm
For I met death before birth;
Fought for life and in reply
Lost my own with a cold despair.
I hugged the fire around the hearth
To warm the heart and wing,
Yet knew the symbol when it came
Lawrence had found the same.
I THREW THE STARLING HARD AS STONE
INTO THE BREAKING EARTH. . . .

DEAD as icebone breaking the hedge,
DEAD as soil failing of good heart.
DEAD as trees quivering with shock,
At the hot death from the plane.

> O the salt loss of life
> Her lovely green ways.
> The emptiness of crib
> And big stare of night.
> The breast of the hills
> Yield a bucket of milk:
> But the crane no longer cries
> With the round birds at dawn
> For the home has been shadowed
> A storm of sorrow drowned the way.

POEM FROM LLANYBRI

If you come my way that is . . .
Between now and then, I will offer you
A fist full of rock cress fresh from the bank
The valley tips of garlic red with dew
Cooler than shallots, a breath you can swank

116

In the village when you come. At noon-day
I will offer you a choice bowl of cawl
Served with a 'lover's' spoon and a chopped spray
Of leeks or savori fach, not used now

In the old way you'll understand. The din
Of children singing through the eyelet sheds
Ringing 'smith hoops, chasing the butt of hens;
Or I can offer you Cwmcelyn spread

With quartz stones, from the wild scratchings of men;
You will have to go carefully with clogs
Or thick shoes for it's treacherous the fen,
The East and West Marshes also have bogs.

Then I'll do the lights, fill the lamp with oil,
Get coal from the shed, water from the well;
Pluck and draw pigeon with crop of green foil
This your good supper from the lime-tree fell.

A sit by the hearth with blue flames rising,
No talk. Just a stare at 'Time' gathering
Healed thoughts, pool insight, like swan sailing
Peace and sound around the home, offering

You a night's rest and my day's energy.
You must come, start this pilgrimage,
Can you come?—send an ode or elegy
In the old way and rise our heritage.

THE CIRCLE OF C

I walk and cinder bats riddle my cloak
I walk to Cwmcelyn ask prophets the way.

There is no way they cried crouched on the hoarstone rock
And the Dogs of Annwn roared louder than of late.

'Red fever will fall with the maytide blossom
   Fever as red as your cloak. Woe to all men.
Food-ties will mellow in the bromide season
      Then willowed peace may be bought.'

      But what of my love I cried
      As a curlew stabbed the sand.

   'And we cut for the answer. They said
He would come not as he said he would come
But later with sailing ice, war-glass and lame
      Grieve not, it is better so.'

      I left the Bay wing-felled and bogged
      Kicked the shale despondent and green

      Heard Rosie say lace-curtained in clogs
      I've put a Yule log on your grate.

BROKEN VOICES

Here a perfect people set—on red rock,
      White and grey as gull met
   Pure to plough, each prince hamlet
   Of slate strong as rate ticket.

Now one mouth twisting twelve tongues—of the flock
      Unlocked the padlocked lungs:
   Slung a trail of steaming dung
   Blocking path of two not sung.

Stained virgin village with dearth:—for the mock
　　Like strumpet jet, rocked mirth
　　And farmer: brought no more worth
　　Than winding sheet of sour berth.

When gossip kneads to grave crust:—with feared shock
　　Runs into fox of dust,
　　Then shall the two minds discussed
　　Remain bold with new sung trust.

ENGLYN

Where poverty strikes pavement—there is found
　　No cripple like contentment
　　Which stultifies all statement
　　Of bright thought from the brain's tent.

THE SEASONS

Spring, which has its appeal in ghosts,
Youth, resurrection, cleansing of the soil
And in dormant roots already considered,
Stirs, with the sharpening of branches
Challenges heart to do that which it cannot,
Sustain overwork, overthought, overlove.
It clears a path for hope: reinstates
Faith, which we had too easily omitted
With death, in the caustic months of the year.

Summer proclaims joy, laughter before its
Arrival: and deceives us into malice
With its non-appearance. It suggests
A romance that we have not received:

Sunny balconies in the mind. The seldom
Forgotten perfect island summer with its
Warm haze on flesh, flower, and hide:
The blossoming of their structure, fragrance
And appeal, from their own root recorded.

Autumn comes strutting in like a cockerel
Red, blue, yellow, and brown. It disintegrates
Our purpose of singular thought: destroys
Relationships: and cuts the sap of pride
Ruthlessly. Those who survive retain their own heart
And voice. Yet autumn with contrawise motion
Shields the creative mind with covering of leaves,
Settles and matures dormant growth which will
Reappear, under the hard skies of spring.

Winter exceeds the year with impunity:
Devours us of all greed: and freezes
That residue. It upholds that which is not:
Which is, the blaze of summer biting
Into our nature for a future reappeal.
Winter intones loss of all things:
Is the next step to death which is loneliness:
Comfort and warmth to be found around our own
Heart and grate, within the steel ribs of this age.

DYLAN THOMAS

POEM

On no work of words now for three lean months in the bloody
Belly of the rich year and the big purse of my body
I bitterly take to task my poverty and craft:

To take to give is all, return what is hungrily given
Puffing the pounds of manna up through the dew to heaven,
The lovely gift of the gab bangs back on a blind shaft.

To lift to leave from the treasures of man is a pleasing death
That will rake at last all currencies of the marked breath
And count the taken, forsaken mysteries in a bad dark.

To surrender now is to pay the expensive ogre twice.
Ancient woods of my blood, dash down to the nut of the seas
If I take to burn or return this world which is each man's work.

POEM

Once it was the colour of saying
Soaked my table the uglier side of a hill
With a capsized field where a school sat still
And a black and white patch of girls grew playing;
The seaslides of saying I must undo
That all the charmingly dead arise to cockcrow and kill.
When I whistled with mitching boys through a reservoir park
Where we stoned at night the cold and cuckoo
Lovers in the dirt of their leafy beds,
The shade of their trees was a word of many shades
And a lamp of lightning for the poor in the dark;
Now my saying shall be my undoing
And every stone I wind off like a reel.

POEM

We lying by seasand, watching yellow
And the grave sea, mock who deride
Who follow the red rivers, hollow
Alcove of words out of cicada shade,

For in this yellow grave of sand and sea
A calling for colour calls with the wind
That's grave and gay as grave and sea
Sleeping on either hand.
The lunar silences, the silent tide
Lapping the still canals, the dry tide-master
Ribbed between desert and water storm,
Should cure our ills of the water
With a one-coloured calm;
The heavenly music over the sand
Sounds with the grains as they hurry
Hiding the golden mountains and mansions
Of the grave, gay seaside land.
Bound by a sovereign strip we lie,
Watch yellow, wish for wind to blow away
The strata of the shore and drown red rock;
But wishes breed not, neither
Can we fend off the rock arrival,
Lie watching yellow until the golden weather
Breaks, O my heart's blood, like a heart and hill.

POEM

The spire cranes. Its statue is an aviary.
From the stone nest it does not let the feathery
Carved birds blunt their striking throats on the salt gravel,
Pierce the spilt sky with diving wing in weed and heel
An inch in froth. Chimes cheat the prison statue, pelter
In time like outlaw rains on that priest, water,
Time for the swimmers' hands, music for silver lock
And mouth. Both note and plume plunge from the spire's
        hook.
Those craning birds are choice for you, songs that jump back
To the built voice, or fly with winter to the bells,
But do not travel down dumb wind like prodigals.

IN MEMORY OF ANN JONES

After the funeral, mule praises, brays
Windshake of sail-shaped ears, muffle-toes tap
Tap happily of one peg in the thick
Grave's foot, blinds down the lids, the teeth in black,
The spittled eyes, the salt ponds in the sleeves,
Morning smack of the spade that wakes up sleep,
Shakes a desolate boy who slits his throat
In the dark of the coffin and shreds dry leaves,
That breaks one bone to light with a judgement clout,
After the feast of tear-stuffed time and thistles
In a room with a stuffed fox and a stale fern,
I stand, for this memorial's sake, alone
In the snivelling hours with dead, humped Ann
Whose hooded fountain heart once fell in puddles
Round the parched worlds of Wales and drowned each sun,
(Though this for her is a monstrous image blindly
Magnified out of praise; her death was a still drop;
She would not have me sinking in the holy
Flood of her heart's flame; she would lie dumb and deep
And need no druid of her broken body.)
But I, Ann's bard on a raised heart, call all
The seas to service that her wood-tongued virtue
Babble like a bellbuoy over the hymning heads,
Bow down the walls of the ferned and foxy woods
That her love sing and swing through a brown chapel,
Bless her bent spirit with four, crossing birds.
Her flesh was meek as milk, but this skyward statue
With the wild breast and blessed and giant skull
Is carved from her in a room with a wet window
In a fiercely mourning house in a crooked year.
I know her scrubbed and sour humble hands
Lie with religion in their cramp, her threadbare
Whisper in a damp word, her wits drilled hollow,
Her fist of a face died clenched on a round pain;

And sculptured Ann is seventy years of stone,
These cloud-sapped, marble hands, this monumental
Argument of the small voice, gesture and psalm
Storm me for ever over her grave until
The stuffed lung of the fox twitch and cry Love
And the strutting fern lay seeds on the black sill.

POEM IN OCTOBER

Especially when the October wind
With frosty fingers punishes my hair,
Caught by the crabbing sun I walk on fire
And cast a shadow crab upon the land,
By the sea's side, hearing the noise of birds,
Hearing the raven cough in winter sticks,
My busy heart who shudders as she talks
Sheds the syllabic blood and drains her words.

Shut, too, in a tower of words, I mark
On the horizon walking like trees
The wordy shapes of women and the rows
Of the star-gestured children in the park.
Some let me make you of the vowelled beeches,
Some of the oaken voices, from the roots
Of many a thorny shire tell you notes,
Some let me make you of the water's speeches.

Behind a pot of ferns the wagging clock
Tells me the hour's word, the neural meaning.
Flies on the shafted disc, declaims the morning
And tells the windy weather in the cock.
Some let me make you of the meadow's signs;
The signal grass that tells me all I know
Breaks with the wormy winter through the eye.
Some let me spell you of the raven's sins.

Especially when the October wind
(Some let me make you of autumnal vowels,
The spider-tongued, and the loud hill of Wales)
With fist of turnips punishes the land,
Some let me make you of the heartless words.
The heart is drained that, spelling in the scurry
Of chemic blood, warned of the coming fury.
By the sea's side hear the dark-vowelled birds.

POEM FOR CAITLIN

(FOR CAITLIN)

I make this in a warring absence when
Each ancient, stone-necked minute of love's season
Harbours my anchored tongue, slips the quaystone,
When, praise is blessed, her pride in mast and fountain
Sailed and set dazzling by the handshaped ocean,
In that proud sailing tree with branches driven
Through the last vault and vegetable groyne,
And this weak house to marrow-columned heaven,

Is corner-cast, breath's rag, scrawled weed, a vain
And opium head, crow stalk, puffed, cut, and blown,
Or like the tide-looped breastknot reefed again
Or rent ancestrally the roped sea-hymen
And, pride is last, is like a child alone
By magnet winds to her blind mother drawn,
Bread and milk mansion in a toothless town.

She makes for me a nettle's innocence
And a silk pigeon's guilt in her proud absence,
In the molested rocks the shell of virgins,
The frank, closed pearl, the sea-girls' lineaments
Is maiden in the shameful oak, omens
Whalebed and bulldance, the gold bush of lions
Proud as a sucked stone and huge as insects.

These are her contraries: the beast who follows
With priest's grave foot and hand of fine assassins
Her molten flight up cinder-nesting columns,
Calls the starved fire herd, is cast in ice,
Lost in a limp-treed and uneating silence,
Who scales a hailing hill in her cold flintsteps
Falls on a ring of summers and locked noons.

I make a weapon of an ass's skeleton
And walk the warring sands by the dead town,
Cudgel great air, wreck east, and topple sundown,
Storm her sped heart, hang with beheaded veins
Its wringing shell, and let her eyelids fasten.
Destruction, picked by birds, brays through the jawbone,
And, for that murder's sake, dark with contagion
Like an approaching wave I sprawl to ruin.

Ruin, the room of errors, one rood dropped
Down the stacked sea and water pillared shade,
Weighed in rock shroud, is my proud pyramid;
Where, wound in emerald linen and sharp wind,
The hero's head lies scraped of every legend,
Comes love's anatomist with sungloved hand
Who picks the live heart on a diamond.

'His mother's womb had a tongue that lapped up mud,'
Cried the topless, inchtaped lips from hank and hood
In that bright anchorground where I lay linened,
'A lizard darting with black venom's thread
Doubled, to fork him back, through the lockjaw bed
And the breath-white, curtained mouth of seed.'
'See,' drummed the taut masks, 'how the dead ascend:
In the groin's endless coil a man is tangled.'

These once-blind eyes have breathed a wind of visions,
The cauldron's root through this once-rindless hand
Fumed like a tree, and tossed a burning bird;
With loud, torn tooth and tail and cobweb drum
The crumpled packs fled by this ghost in bloom,
And, mild as pardon from a cloud of pride,
The terrible world my brother bares his skins.

Now in the cloud's big breast lie quiet countries,
Delivered seas my love from her proud place
Walks with no wound, no lightning in her face,
A calm wind blows that raised the trees like hair
Once where the soft snow's blood was turned to ice.
And though my love pulls the pale, nippled air,
Prides of to-morrow suckling in her eyes,
Yet this I make in a forgiving presence.

ORMOND THOMAS

STRANGE WITHIN THE DIVIDING ...

Sensation of the birth beat, softer
    than calm-brushed bracken in winter,
Regular in its closeness, fertile
    in the beauty and warmth of potentiality.
No still-born laughter, no empty smile
    faces the need for the swift pity.
With a background not found in a brothel
but with the support of ages
    painted with deft brush in the pages
    of the never-ending revolution of the wheel
that is everlasting in its solidity.

Strange within the dividing of blood-lines
   the doubt of a relegation of spirit is born,
The wet moonlit grasses with their tasteless wines
   wait for to-morrow and the dawn,
While the hollow questions have echoed through sleep,
   On, plunging down past colourless green,
   Towards the raining morning,
   in which with its grey half-mourning
Now as always they will keep
   asking the clutching, Where have we been?
      Where have we been?

Always the night has covered the track,
   tossing the traces with the blue cloud sand
Taking love's twigs and heather in her dark hand
and making a new bed in the low rock,
   Under whose shadow with their cold walk
   they may hide the straw enclosed leaf,
Red with the blood of unfathomable grief
   Holding up towards the hanging branch a brow
   wet with the eagerness of the creation
      and again cooling with the vow
   pledging the war of condemnation.
Never to be forgotten, only to break
   with the ultimate gain of freedom's sake.

LET US BREAK DOWN THE BARRIERS...

Let us break down the barriers of crying.
Tears cannot stretch forth their fingers
Far enough down from the shadow
Into the sunlight to grasp the trouble.
They are blistered and evaporated
Leaving no mark, and not touching
The ache that made us weep.

It is but in the crucible of meeting
In which compounded are the salts:
And happens the crystallization of issues:
That longing is caught in the prism of the eye,
Is split up for us to see,
Is refracted out, and continues.
We are as before, except
That we have seen carved in light
For a sharp-edged moment in the sun
The nucleus of our existence, of our purpose.

If for a moment the emotion of the whole
Of all quick-thinking elements of time
Is caught within the starlit instant's glance,
Your tears are futile
As the apple blossom in the wind,
And as insecure as the ripples
Left on the shore by the tide.

Yet I understand the mysteries of ages
Through the circle of a young child's pity.

Feed them the moment, and your unborn child
And clean the corroding water.
Strengthen the chain's link
And weld the whole around the earth . . .

You will not break for there runs
Throughout the flowers
A wire unbreakable in all eras of space.

POEM IN FEBRUARY

Walking besides the lank sea-shore in February
with the faint birdmarks, triangular,
and the grave curve and cry of the whirlpool bay,
I set a line the wave cannot destroy,

wave turning upon the dunes, beyond the rock
first searched and sought out by the renewing tide
that leaves no hidden sanctuary.

The line is valid as a winter dream; upon no rack of logic,
under the point of nails, proving some non-existence
of a spirit by a manrib cracking before pain;
it is no wreck of ghostship on the shore,
gone in the daylight, only there on moon;

so when the reedwinds come to seek me out
my hair is seagrass, fingers sand,
and over all the watermarks they pass;
there is no enemy; here is friend.

The slender sun combing the grey hair's cloud
drops the insistent shadow on the distant castle;
broken like bone. Yet on the beach the skull's no alien,
and the black woods around above witness no burial
of the dead seas. They are not alone

for under them all and the leafmoulds, and the waters
through the late winter boughs, and under the stones,
the skull and I are handlocked like a flood,
a flood in February when first the primrose breaks.

Three Cliffs Bay.

R. S. THOMAS

A PEASANT

Iago Prytherch his name, though, be it allowed,
Just an ordinary man of the bald Welsh hills,
Who pens a few sheep in a gap of cloud.

130

Docking mangels, chipping the green skin
From the yellow bones with a half-witted grin
Of satisfaction, or churning the crude earth
To a stiff sea of clods, that glint in the wind—
So are his days spent, his spittled mirth
Rarer than the sun, that cracks the cheeks
Of the gaunt sky perhaps once in a week.
And then at night see him fixed in his chair
Motionless, except when he leans to gob in the fire.
There is something frightening in the vacancy of his mind.
His clothes, sour with years of sweat
And animal contact, shock the refined,
But affected, sense with their stark naturalness.
Yet this is your prototype, who, season by season,
Against siege of rain and the wind's attrition
Preserves his stock, an impregnable fortress
Not to be stormed even in death's confusion.
Remember him, then, for he, too, is a winner of wars,
Enduring like a tree under the curious stars.

THE QUESTION

Who is skilled to read
The strange epitaph of the salt weed
Scrawled on our shores? Who can make plain
The thin, dark characters of rain,
Or the hushed speech of wind and star
In the deep-throated fir?
Was not this the voice that lulled
Job's seething mind to a still calm,
Yet tossed his heart to the racked world?

HENRY TREECE

SECOND COMING 1942

Under the hill the old horse stands
Away from the wind,
Waiting a second coming.
The timid flock together by the wall
Cough and slip back into their dream
Of meadow-lands where knife was never known.

The old man clasps his tired hands
And seems to find
No labour worth the doing.
The rusty bucket jangles at the well,
And memories rush into the room
Of the lost son who is to be reborn.

IN THE BEGINNING WAS THE BIRD

In the beginning was the bird,
A spume of feathers on the face of time,
Man's model for destruction, God's defence.

Before man, a bird, a feather before time,
And music growing outward into space,
The feathered shears cutting dreams in air.

Before birds, a God, a Nothing with a shape
More horrible than mountains or the Plague,
A Voice as large as fate, a tongue of bronze.

Before this, O no before was there.
Where? Among the placeless atoms, mad
As tale the maggot makes locked in the skull.

And so I state a bird. For sanity
My brain's lips blow the tumbled plume.
I see it prophesy the path winds take.

THE CRIMSON CHERRY TREE

There is no sweeter sight, I swear, in Heaven
Than blossom on the cherry trees by Clee.
Ah dainty brides, you dance on through my dreams
And in the town bring memory of a breeze
That blew from Corvedale, across the valley that
Must have run red with agony when Owen spoke,
Torturing the air about his council-chair
With shapes of fiery dragons flaming, wolves
That ran through city gates to bring despair
Upon the tow-haired marchers, tearing sheep
And leaving foul the water-holes. I feel
The failure of a people when that wind
Howls through my heart and shows me Caradoc
Heaped high with lads who should have brought their songs
Right to the walls of Ludlow, over Severn,
Regaining the green pastures with a word.

Ah, cherry-tree, so lissom in the wind,
Matter for poets and the love-sick mad,
I see your virgin blossom splashed with blood,
Bright red against the white, and at your feet
The gentle lord who walked without a sword,
Believing tales of peace among the hills,
Trusting the word, the signatory name,
Forgetting the black seasons of a race.

Y DDRAIG GOCH

The dragon of our dreams roared in the hills
That ring the sunlit land of children's songs.
Red with the lacquer of a fairy-tale,
His fiery breath fried all besieging knights.
Whole seasons could he lay the land in waste
By puffing once upon the standing corn!

He was our dragon dressed in red, who kept
Sly ghosts from lurking underneath the thatch,
And made the hen lay dark-brown eggs for tea.
One word to him, just as you went to bed,
Made Twm, the postman, call next afternoon;
'Ho, bachgen,' That is what he'd say, 'Just look,
A fine blue postal-order from your Mam!
Twm gets a pint for bring that, I bet!'

The dragon cured us when the measles came,
And let the mare drop me a coal-black foal.
He taught us where nests lay, and found us fish,
Then thawed the snow to save the winter lamb.

Ho, Ddraig Goch, my pretty, pretty friend!
We were his children, knowing all his ways;
We laid out nightly gifts beneath the hedge,
Five linnet's eggs, a cup, a broken whip,
And heard his gracious sighs sweep through the trees.
But tears for all the fools who called him false!
One lad who sniggered fell down Parry's well;
The English Parson had a plague of warts;
Old Mrs. Hughes was bitten by a cat;
The school roof fell in when the teacher smiled!

Ho, Ddraig Goch, they tell me you are dead;
They say they heard you weeping in the hills
For all your children gone to London Town.
They say your tears set Tawe in a flood.

I'm older now, but still I like to think
Of your great glass-green eyes fixed on the Fferm,
Guarding the children, keeping them from harm.

Don't die, old dragon, wait a few years more,
I shall come back and bring you boys to love.

MEURIG WALTERS

RHONDDA

Below, Ferndale squats in a gash of cwm,
its trellised streets spat from a tube of road
that crashes through: streets huddling fire from cliques,
coloned by chapels and commaed by pubs
and cinemas inoculating soul—
silicosed men against the hate-red cough
of discontent and breathless war for food.
Flanked by moon-greased eggs of mountain sprawled tense
to chest a sore back of sky, sore as tense,
and harsh unnippled breasts of tip, and pins
of stack that belch but air, spued belly-cold.
Its houses gummed together like a toy,
glum and squint, munching their cud of hate,
all alike like Siamese polyplet cats,
but a varied drabness labelling their eyes.
The rows converge like half-a-cart-wheel spokes
upon the Strand where hill is wall-steep dam
against the overflow of valley streets,
and but a thread of road drawn taut, drawn down
from little Moscow up beyond the hills.

SEMINARY

Here there are men who vomit words
and make an art of bumping heads
against the Citadel of God,
and bump the bruise to numb the pain.

Obese with thought, they sprawl and watch
God bubbling in the mind's retort,
and check their graphs by tests supplied
by Brunner, Berdyaev and Barth.

They thumb the leaves of yellow books.
Their backs crook with the sack of thoughts
they pilfer from the bins of men
who kept an open house for God.

VERNON WATKINS

LLEWELYN'S CHARIOT

Sun of all suns, seed of dandelion seeds,
Sprung from the stem of delight and the starry course,
High at the helm of night, in the van of deeds,
A one-wheeled carriage you drive and a headless horse.
Your Maker makes you his glory, you grasp and push
Through bars the bugle, the mirror, the string of beads,
The doll and the wooden men; with a mighty wish
You ride the brunt of creation's galloping beds.

What golden fleece enshrines at the very prow
Your marvelling head, and summons from ancient seas
Sailors toiling, under the black sea-crow,
What ever-moving, miraculous, wind-faint fleece;

But you kick those puppets, those men of deeds, through the
      bars,
The tossed men lost, the lost men under the ark,
Seed of spray's seed, swept from the flight of the stars
To a point of light in your look that is almost dark.

Rameses, trumpet and chariot, all you outrun
Grasping your cage where grief is banished for good,
Created nothing, timeless, perpetual one
Dropped from light-years to crawl under legs of wood,
Star-seed, breath-downed, dropped from the topmost sun
To the toppling house near the shed that shadows a hearse,
From whirling, luminous night, to sleep here alone
In the darkness a great light leaves, where a feather stirs.

And I, your listener, stopped on the stairway of breath,
Awake, in the stranger's bed, in the cold, high room,
Calling the sea from Leviathan hollows of earth,
I watch them, castaway toys, while you drive and boom
Your course in the cot to my bed, with the speed of ice,
The giant mirror, the trumpet ringed with a bell,
Till naked you stand, gold-fleeced, shaping, a shell,
All seas to your colour, Llewelyn, child above price.

THE SUNBATHER

Inert he lies on the saltgold sand
And sees through his lids the scarlet sky.
The sea will run back if he breathes a sigh.
He can hide the sun with a roselit hand.

Loitering, he crossed the shingle-shore
Where his eyes looked back at the glint of shells.
With a quoit of stone he startled the bells
That sleep in the rocks' vibrating core.

Thought-blind to the chosen place he passed.
The seagulls rose, and circled, and dropped;
And there, throwing down his coat, he stopped.
He, touching the mould of the world, lies fast.

The noon-sun dodges around his knee.
The sand at his head now trembles pale
The wind at his temples carries a tale
And before him flies the bewildered sea.

The sun, the sea and the wind are three.
But he narrows them down with a dreaming eye.
With his hands at rest and his drawn-up thigh
He can imagine the sacred tree.

For a point of light has seeded all
And the beautiful seed has come to rest
For a sunblown moment in his breast,
A tree where the leaves will never fall.

'Come back. You were with us ages ago.
We have thrown your bones to the carrion gull.
To the dripping cave we have sold your skull,
And the delicate flower which was born to blow

Is lost in the flow of the marble sea.
We have made seaweeds out of your locks
And your star-white bones in the vaulted rocks
Lie broken and cold, like shells in the scree.'

So Shades converse, and the world's dumb thud
Muffles their argument. Man, more strong
Gives, to console their frightened song,
The beat that consoles them most, his blood.

THE COLLIER

When I was born on Amman hill
A dark bird crossed the sun.
Sharp on the floor the shadow fell;
I was the youngest son.

And when I went to the County School
I worked in a shaft of light.
In the wood of the desk I cut my name:
Dai for Dynamite.

The tall black hills my brothers stood;
Their lessons all were done.
From the door of the school when I ran out
They frowned to watch me run.

The slow grey bells they rung a chime
Surly with grief or age.
Clever or clumsy, lad or lout,
All would look for a wage,

I learnt the valley flowers' names
And the rough bark knew my knees.
I brought home trout from the river
And spotted eggs from the trees.

A coloured coat I was given to wear
Where the lights of the rough land shone.
Still jealous of my favour
The tall black hills looked on.

They dipped my coat in the blood of a kid
And they cast me down a pit,
And although I crossed with strangers
There was no way up from it.

Soon as I went from the County School
I worked in a shaft. Said Jim,
'You will get your chain of gold, my lad,
But not for a likely time.'

And one said, 'Jack was not raised up
When the wind blew out the light
Though he interpreted their dreams
And guessed their fears by night.'

And Tom, he shivered his leper's lamp
For the strain that round him grew;
And I heard mouths pray in the after-damp
When the picks would not break through.

They changed words there in darkness
And still through my head they run,
And white on my limbs is the linen sheet
And gold on my neck the sun.

THE DEAD WORDS

So flies love's meteor to her shroud of winds.
The crisp words couch in their last battling-place
Where widowed silence, threaded like black lace,
Held a dumb minute, stabs the dark like pins.
It is so breathless. There the fire begins
To seed, we know not how. There blows the race
Of spirits, and they watch the stiff leaves brace
With last look backward to the town of sins.
There clenches the close fist through wreath and wraith
The sooted page where wrought like golden wire
The sly words glitter with an angel's breath;
Love's moistening seal is mastered there entire,
And the wind proves, where they are dressed for death,
Cinders are priestlike in their tale of fire.

SYCAMORE

O, I am green and fair:
Is there a fairer tree?
Who is it underneath
Sleeps the sleep of death?
There is no answer there.
There is no answer there.

Centuries made me firm.
Far I have spread my roots.
I grip the flying stream.
Aching, I drop my fruits.
Who is it sleeps below?
Who is it sleeps below?

My wood made long ago
Lutes of true, hollow sound.
Lovers still carve them out
Above this burial-mound.
Who is it sleeps below?
Who is it sleeps below?

Who sleeps? The young streams feed
My boughs. The blind keys spin.
Hark, he is dead indeed.
Never shall fall again
My natural, winged seed
On this small-statured man.

RETURNING TO GOLEUFRYN

Returning to my grandfather's house, after this exile
From the coracle-river, long left with a coin to be good,
Returning with husks of those venturing ears for food
To lovely Carmarthen, I touch and remember the turnstile

Of this death-bound river. Fresh grass. Here I find that crown
In the shadow of dripping river-wood; then look up to the burn-
    ing mile
Of windows. It is Goleufryn, the house on the hill;
And picking a child's path in a turn of the Towy I meet the
    prodigal town.

Sing, little house, clap hands: shut, like a book of the Psalms,
On the leaves and pressed flowers of a journey. All is sunny
In the garden behind you. The soil is alive with blind-petalled
    blooms
Plundered by bees. Gooseberries and currants are gay
With tranquil, unsettled light. Breathless light begging alms
Of the breathing grasses bent over the river of tombs
Flashes. A salmon has swallowed the tribute-money
Of the path. On the farther bank I see ragged urchins play

With thread and pin. O lead me that I may drown
In those earlier cobbles, reflected; a street that is strewn with
    palms,
Rustling with blouses and velvet. Yet I alone
By the light in the sunflower deepening, here stand, my eyes
    cast down
To the footprint of accusations, and hear the faint, leavening
Music of first Welsh words; that gust of plumes
'They shall mount up like eagles', dark-throated assumes,
Cold-sunned, low thunder and gentleness of the authentic
    Throne.

Yet now I am lost, lost in the water-wound looms
Where brief, square windows break on a garden's decay.
Gold butter is shining, the tablecloth speckled with crumbs.
The kettle throbs. In the calendar harvest is shown,
Standing in sheaves. Which way would I do you wrong?
Low, crumbling doorway of the infirm to the mansions of
    evening,

And poor, shrunken furrow where the potatoes are sown,
I shall not unnumber one soul I have stood with and known
To regain your stars struck by horses, your sons of God break-
　　ing in song.

FROM MY LOITERING

From my loitering as a child
In paving-square and field
And from my stone-still tongue
Time is unsealed.

The ages are unstrung
By water from a Triton flung
And the world finds its heart
Which was not always young.

I cannot tell what art
Set the grave spring to start
In whose old pipe and stop
Time plays no part.

But where green eyes look up,
Eyes that are blind with sun,
Uncertain fingers grope
Around the vine-leaved cup.

There little children run
And climb the singing stone
And their sweet dialect
Is learnt by none.

Shadows and leaves infect
The brooding intellect
Beneath whose tongueless wave
Those lives are wrecked.

But they low music have
Winding and gold and grave.
Time's measure they can set
By light, by love.

And in the sun-thrown jet:
'Sweet moment, sweet!' and 'sweeter yet!'
Cry, make the foiled eyes clear,
The parched lips wet.

GEORGE WOODCOCK

LANDORE

Fume-bitten no-grassness of mountains,
Barrenness synthetic—not of drought's summer,
Mean the reek of copper rising through the valley,
Seeping into houses, drying child lungs, eating the cheek of
    beauty,
But keeping factories prosperous, bringing
Dividends to the rentiers, to the workers
Bread in the belly, surcease from absolute want, a little pleasure.

But now the down of grass sprouts, now the fire galvanic
Bursts the yellow flowers, now harsh green
New moss veins the stone brows,
Now birds return to live and feed on the mountain,
Hunger is in the valley, dereliction
Of sag-roof factory and plumeless stack,
Children suffering now the flaccid unfed belly,
Youths squatting for talk in the lee of walls,
The slow aimless round of mountain and stone-grey street,
Pitch-and-toss on the slag heap, walks by the scummed river
And the public library now and again of a morning.

STEEL VALLEY, 1938

War husks its rumours, and the yellow scurf
Of gorse scabs mountains over men who smote
Steel and trod surer feet on slag than turf.

But in their valley, where the fume clouds float
Only in memory and past-praising speech,
These men have learnt life to a meagre rote,

Achieve negation, but no wider reach
Span towards anger. Theirs the needy urge
That prompts the searching of the hungry leech

And tilts the sunning cups of dingy spurge,
Theirs the blunt memory of singeing blast
And prosperous creeping of the slag tip's verge.

Essentials only, cold and hunger, last.
Here stand no idols for iconoclast.

MERTHYRMAWR

Sunday evening. The thick-lipped men binoculared
Steal through the geometric groves of pines,
Observing the steady and fatal hands of poachers
And the young loving in wrinkles of the dunes.

Grey in the wind sand tides against the turrets,
And watchful sight is bridged towards the sea,
Where silent the marram defends a wearing land
And the seagulls climb like Junkers a plaster sky.

The air is alive with voices, the loving whisper,
The rodent scream at neck-constricting hand,
Gulls' earthless wail and dank watchers' laughter.
Always the wind whistles through teeth of sand.

145

Night falls on the lovers, marram and voices.
Dark hinders eyes, yet aids the brutal hand.
Watchers depart, but the snares are filling.
Wind dries the blood on the moving sand.

SOUTHERNDOWN BEACH

Fluid ebon masses, flow
sculptured waves to broken snow
and, speedwell-eyed, delphinium blue,
sky to sea cleaves. Gleaming, new,
of cosmic conjugation born
clouds from the faint horizon spawn,
rise on the landward wing, impart
misgivings to the tripper's heart
and, hundred-browed, attack the sun.
Dancer's feet of ripples spin
up the firm sand. The swimmers glide
beachward on the swelling tide.